THE

PROSTRATE STATE:

SOUTH CAROLINA UNDER NEGRO GOVERNMENT.

BY

JAMES S. PIKE,

LATE MINISTER OF THE UNITED STATES AT THE HAGUE.

NEW YORK:

D. APPLETON AND COMPANY,
549 & 551 BROADWAY,
1874.

PREFACE.

THE following pages were written in South Carolina, during the session of the Legislature, in the months of February and March, 1873. They take their coloring from the scenes by which the writer was surrounded. This explanation is necessary, to account for the form in which a portion of the contents is presented.

I have no positive theory in regard to the future of South Carolina. Fifteen years ago, when emancipation seemed distant, I ventured the prediction that the Gulf States would finally have to be surrendered to the blacks; but the abolition of slavery having been suddenly precipitated, the conditions of the problem have become changed. Yet there are those who believe such is now the inevitable fate of several of the Southern States, South Carolina included. In the following pages I have combated this sentiment as regards South Carolina, and have pointed out the

method by which it seems to me its Africanization can be prevented, and suggested some of the
considerations which should inspire an effort to
prevent such a result. But it may turn out that
there is a wide difference between what can be
done and what will be done. The white people
of South Carolina may permit what they might
prevent. The decision of the case rests mainly
with them. But their course in the present crisis
of their fortunes is not a matter of interest to
themselves alone; it deeply concerns the people
of the other States, and it is their attention that
I invoke to the following exposition. The facts
challenge the thoughtful consideration of every
man who does not believe that our political system can stand any thing and defy any thing.

NEW YORK, *Oct.*, 1873.

CONTENTS.

CHAPTER VII.

CHAPTER VIII.

CHAPTER IX.

CHAPTER X.

CHAPTER XI.

CHAPTER XII.

CHAPTER XIII.

CHAPTER XIV.

THE PROSTRATE STATE.

CHAPTER I.

COLUMBIA, the capital of South Carolina, is charmingly situated in the heart of the upland country, near the geographical centre of the State. It has broad, open streets, regularly laid out, and fine, shady residences in and about the town. The opportunity for rides and drives can hardly be surpassed. There are good animals and good turnouts to be seen on the streets at all times; and now, in midwinter, the weather invites to such displays. It seems there was a little real winter here at Christmas and New Year's, when the whole country suffered such an excess of sudden cold. There was even skating and sleighing for a week. But now there is no frost, and the recollection of it is dispelled by the genial spring weather that prevails.

Yesterday, about 4 P. M., the assembled wisdom of the State, whose achievements are illustrated on that theatre, issued forth from the State-House. About three-quarters of the crowd belonged to the African race. They were of every hue, from the light octoroon to the deep black. They were such a looking body of men as might pour out of a market-house or a court-house at random in any Southern State. Every negro type and physiognomy was here to be seen, from the genteel serving-man to the rough-hewn customer from the rice or cotton field. Their dress was as varied as their countenances. There was the second-hand black frock-coat of infirm gentility, glossy and threadbare. There was the stove-pipe hat of many ironings and departed styles. There was also to be seen a total disregard of the proprieties of costume in the coarse and dirty garments of the field; the stub-jackets and slouch hats of soiling labor. In some instances, rough woolen comforters embraced the neck and hid the absence of linen. Heavy brogans, and short, torn trousers, it was impossible to hide. The dusky tide flowed out into the littered and barren grounds, and, issuing through the coarse wooden fence of the inclosure, melted away into the street beyond. These were the legislators of South Carolina.

In conspicuous bass-relief over the door of exit,

on the panels of the stately edifice, the marble visages of George McDuffie and Robert Y. Hayne overlooked the scene. Could they veritably witness it from their dread abode? What then? "I tremble," wrote Jefferson, when depicting the character of Southern slavery, "I tremble when I reflect that God is just." But did any of that old band of Southern Revolutionary patriots who wrestled in their souls with the curse of slavery ever contemplate such a descent into barbarism as this spectacle implied and typified? "My God, look at this!" was the unbidden ejaculation of a low-country planter, clad in homespun, as he leaned over the rail inside the House, gazing excitedly upon the body in session. "This is the first time I have been here. I thought I knew what we were doing when we consented to emancipation. I knew the negro, and I predicted much that has happened, but I never thought it would come to this. Let me go."

Here, then, is the outcome, the ripe, perfected fruit of the boasted civilization of the South, after two hundred years of experience. A white community, that had gradually risen from small beginnings, till it grew into wealth, culture, and refinement, and became accomplished in all the arts of civilization; that successfully asserted its resistance to a foreign tyranny by deeds of conspicuous valor, which achieved liberty and

independence through the fire and tempest of
civil war, and illustrated itself in the councils of
the nation by orators and statesmen worthy of
any age or nation—such a community is then reduced to this.   It lies prostrate in the dust, ruled.
over by this strange conglomerate, gathered from
the ranks of its own servile population.   It is the
spectacle of a society suddenly turned bottom-
side up.   The wealth, the intelligence, the culture, the wisdom of the State, have broken
through the crust of that social volcano on which
they were contentedly reposing, and have sunk
out of sight, consumed by the subterranean fires
they had with such temerity braved and defied.

In the place of this old aristocratic society
stands the rude form of the most ignorant democracy that mankind ever saw, invested with the
functions of government.   It is the dregs of the
population habilitated in the robes of their intelligent predecessors, and asserting over them the
rule of ignorance and corruption, through the in-
exorable machinery of a majority of numbers.   It
is barbarism overwhelming civilization by physical force.   It is the slave rioting in the halls of
his master, and putting that master under his
feet.   And, though it is done without malice and
without vengeance, it is nevertheless none the
less completely and absolutely done.   Let us approach nearer and take a closer view.   We will

enter the House of Representatives. Here sit one
hundred and twenty-four members. Of these,
twenty-three are white men, representing the remains of the old civilization. These are good-
looking, substantial citizens. They are men of
weight and standing in the communities they
represent. They are all from the hill country.
The frosts of sixty and seventy winters whiten
the heads of some among them. There they sit,
grim and silent. They feel themselves to be but
loose stones, thrown in to partially obstruct a
current they are powerless to resist. They say
little and do little as the days go by. They simply watch the rising tide, and mark the progres-
sive steps of the inundation. They hold their
places reluctantly. They feel themselves to be
in some sort martyrs, bound stoically to suffer in
behalf of that still great element in the State
whose prostrate fortunes are becoming the sport
of an unpitying Fate. Grouped in a corner of the
commodious and well-furnished chamber, they
stolidly survey the noisy riot that goes on in the
great black Left and Centre, where the business
and debates of the House are conducted, and
where sit the strange and extraordinary guides
of the fortunes of a once proud and haughty
State. In this crucial trial of his pride, his manhood, his prejudices, his spirit, it must be said of
the Southern Bourbon of the Legislature that he

comports himself with a dignity, a reserve, and a decorum, that command admiration. He feels that the iron hand of Destiny is upon him. He is gloomy, disconsolate, hopeless. The gray heads of this generation openly profess that they look for no relief. They see no way of escape. The recovery of influence, of position, of control in the State, is felt by them to be impossible. They accept their position with a stoicism that promises no reward here or hereafter. They are the types of a conquered race. They staked all and lost all. Their lives remain, their property and their children do not. War, emancipation, and grinding taxation, have consumed them. Their struggle now is against complete confiscation. They endure, and wait for the night.

This dense negro crowd they confront do the debating, the squabbling, the law-making, and create all the clamor and disorder of the body. These twenty-three white men are but the observers, the enforced auditors of the dull and clumsy imitation of a deliberative body, whose appearance in their present capacity is at once a wonder and a shame to modern civilization.

Deducting the twenty-three members referred to, who comprise the entire strength of the opposition, we find one hundred and one remaining. Of this one hundred and one, ninety-four are colored, and seven are their white allies. Thus the

blacks outnumber the whole body of whites in
the House more than three to one. On the mere
basis of numbers in the State the injustice of this
disproportion is manifest, since the black population is relatively four to three of the whites. A
just rectification of the disproportion, on the
basis of population merely, would give fifty-four
whites to seventy black members. And the line
of race very nearly marks the line of hostile politics. As things stand, the body is almost literally a Black Parliament, and it is the only one
on the face of the earth which is the representative
of a white constituency and the professed expo-
nent of an advanced type of modern civilization.
But the reader will find almost any portraiture
inadequate to give a vivid idea of the body, and
enable him to comprehend the complete meta-
morphosis of the South Carolina Legislature,
without observing its details. The Speaker is
black, the Clerk is black, the door-keepers are
black, the little pages are black, the chairman
of the Ways and Means is black. and the chaplain is coal-black. At some of the desks sit colored men whose types it would be hard to find
outside of Congo; whose costume, visages, atti-
tudes, and expression, only befit the forecastle
of a buccaneer. It must be remembered, also,
that these men, with not more than half a dozen
exceptions, have been themselves slaves, and

that their ancestors were slaves for generations.
Recollecting the report of the famous schooner
Wanderer, fitted out by a Southern slave-holder
twelve or fifteen years ago, in ostentatious defi-
ance of the laws against the slave-trade, and
whose owner and master boasted of having
brought a cargo of slaves from Africa and safely
landed them in South Carolina and Georgia, one
thinks it must be true, and that some of these
representatives are the very men then stolen from
their African homes. If this be so, we will not
now quarrel over their presence. It would be one
of those extraordinary coincidences that would of
itself almost seem to justify the belief of the direct
interference of the hand of Providence in the affairs of men.

CHAPTER II.

The Negro as a Legislator.—His Fluency in Debate.—Earnestness and Good-Humor his Characteristics.—The Future of the State.

ONE of the things that first strike a casual observer in this negro assembly is the fluency of debate, if the endless chatter that goes on there can be dignified with this term. The leading topics of discussion are all well understood by the members, as they are of a practical character, and appeal directly to the personal interests of every legislator, as well as to those of his constituents. When an appropriation bill is up to raise money to catch and punish the Ku-klux, they know exactly what it means. They feel it in their bones. So, too, with educational measures. The free school comes right home to them; then the business of arming and drilling the black militia. They are eager on this point. Sambo can talk on these topics and those of a kindred character, and their endless ramifications, day in and day out. There is no end to his gush and babble. The intellectual level is that of a bevy of fresh

converts at a negro camp-meeting. Of course
this kind of talk can be extended indefinitely. It
is the doggerel of debate, and not beyond the
reach of the lowest parts. Then the negro is
imitative in the extreme. He can copy like a
parrot or a monkey, and he is always ready for
a trial of his skill. He believes he can do any
thing, and never loses a chance to try, and is just
as ready to be laughed at for his failure as ap-
plauded for his success. He is more vivacious
than the white, and, being more volatile and good-
natured, he is correspondingly more irrepressible.
His misuse of language in his imitations is at
times ludicrous beyond measure. He notoriously
loves a joke or an anecdote, and will burst into a
broad guffaw on the smallest provocation. He
breaks out into an incoherent harangue on the
floor just as easily, and being without practice,
discipline, or experience, and wholly oblivious of
Lindley Murray, or any other restraint on compo-
sition, he will go on repeating himself, dancing as
it were to the music of his own voice, forever.
He will speak half a dozen times on one question,
and every time say the same things without
knowing it. He answers completely to the description of a stupid speaker in Parliament, given
by Lord Derby on one occasion. It was said of
him that he did not know what he was going to
say when he got up; he did not know what he

was saying while he was speaking, and he did not know what he had said when he sat down.

But the old stagers admit that the colored brethren have a wonderful aptness at legislative proceedings. They are "quick as lightning" at detecting points of order, and they certainly make incessant and extraordinary use of their knowledge. No one is allowed to talk five minutes without interruption, and one interruption is the signal for another and another, until the original speaker is smothered under an avalanche of them. Forty questions of privilege will be raised in a day. At times, nothing goes on but alternating questions of order and of privilege. The inefficient colored friend who sits in the Speaker's chair cannot suppress this extraordinary element of the debate. Some of the blackest members exhibit a pertinacity of intrusion in raising these points of order and questions of privilege that few white men can equal. Their struggles to get the floor, their bellowings and physical contortions, baffle description. The Speaker's hammer plays a perpetual tattoo all to no purpose. The talking and the interruptions from all quarters go on with the utmost license. Every one esteems himself as good as his neighbor, and puts in his oar, apparently as often for love of riot and confusion as for any thing else. It is easy to imagine what are his ideas

of propriety and dignity among a crowd of his own
color, and these are illustrated without reserve.
The Speaker orders a member whom he has discovered to be particularly unruly to take his seat.
The member obeys, and with the same motion
that he sits down, throws his feet on to his desk,
hiding himself from the Speaker by the soles of
his boots. In an instant he appears again on the
floor. After a few experiences of this sort, the
Speaker threatens, in a laugh, to call " the gem-
man " to order. This is considered a capital joke,
and a guffaw follows. The laugh goes round, and
then the peanuts are cracked and munched faster
than ever ; one hand being employed in fortifying
the inner man with this nutriment of universal
use, while the other enforces the views of the
orator. This laughing propensity of the sable
crowd is a great cause of disorder. They laugh
as hens cackle—one begins and all follow.

But underneath all this shocking burlesque
upon legislative proceedings, we must not forget
that there is something very real to this uncouth
and untutored multitude. It is not all sham, nor
all burlesque. They have a genuine interest and
a genuine earnestness in the business of the assembly which we are bound to recognize and
respect, unless we would be accounted shallow
critics. They have an earnest purpose, born of
a conviction that their position and condition

are not fully assured, which lends a sort of dignity to their proceedings. The barbarous, animated jargon in which they so often indulge is on occasion seen to be so transparently sincere and weighty in their own minds that sympathy supplants disgust. The whole thing is a wonderful novelty to them as well as to observers. Seven years ago these men were raising corn and cotton under the whip of the overseer. To-day they are raising points of order and questions of privilege. They find they can raise one as well as the other. They prefer the latter. It is easier, and better paid. Then, it is the evidence of an accomplished result. It means escape and defense from old oppressors. It means liberty. It means the destruction of prison-walls only too real to them. It is the sunshine of their lives. It is their day of jubilee. It is their long-promised vision of the Lord God Almighty.

Shall we, then, be too critical over the spectacle? Perhaps we might more wisely wonder that they can do so well in so short a time. The barbarians overran Rome. The dark ages followed. But then the day finally broke, and civilization followed. The days were long and weary; but they came to an end at last. Now we have the printing-press, the railroad, the telegraph; and these denote an utter revolution in the affairs of mankind. Years may now accomplish what it for-

merly took ages to achieve. Under the new
lights and influences shall not the black man
speedily emerge? Who knows? We may fear,
but we may hope. Nothing in our day is impossible. Take the contested supposition that South
Carolina is to be Africanized. We have a Federal Union of great and growing States. It is in-
contestably white at the centre. We know it to
possess vital powers. It is well abreast of all
modern progress in ideas and improvements. Its
influence is all-pervading. How can a State of
the Union escape it? South Carolina alone, if
left to herself, might fall into midnight darkness.
Can she do it while she remains an integral part
of the nation?

But will South Carolina be Africanized? That
depends. Let us hear the judgment of an intelligent foreigner who has long lived in the South,
and who was here when the war began. He does
not believe it. White people from abroad are
drifting in, bad as things are. Under freedom
the blacks do not multiply as in slavery. The
pickaninnies die off from want of care. Some
blacks are coming in from North Carolina and
Virginia, but others are going off farther South.
The white young men who were growing into
manhood did not seem inclined to leave their
homes and migrate to foreign parts. There was
an exodus after the war, but it has stopped, and

many have come back. The old slave-holders still hold their lands. The negroes were poor and unable to buy, even if the land-owners would sell. This was a powerful impediment to the development of the negro into a controlling force in the State. His whole power was in his numbers. The present disproportion of four blacks to three whites in the State he believed was already decreasing. The whites seemed likely to more than hold their own, while the blacks would fall off. Cumulative voting would encourage the growth and add to the political power of the whites in the Legislature, where they were at present over-slaughed.

Then the manufacturing industry was growing in magnitude and vitality. This spread various new employments over the State, and every one became a centre to invite white immigration. This influence was already felt. Trade was increased in the towns, and this meant increase of white population. High taxes were a detriment and a drag. But the trader put them on to his goods, and the manufacturer on to his products, and made the consumer pay.

But this important question cannot be dismissed in a paragraph. It requires further treatment. It involves the fortunes of the State far too deeply, and the duties of the white people and the interests of the property-holder, are too intimately connected with a just decision of it, to excuse a hasty or shallow judgment. We must defer its further consideration to another occasion. It is the question which is all in all to South Carolina.

CHAPTER III.

THE corruption of the State government of South Carolina is a topic that has grown threadbare in the handling. The last administration stole right hand and left with a recklessness and audacity without parallel. The robbers under it embraced all grades of people. The thieves had to combine to aid one another. It took a combination of the principal authorities to get at the Treasury, and they had to share the plunder alike. All the smaller fry had their proportions, the legislators and lobbymen included. The principal men of the Scott administration are living in Columbia, and nobody undertakes to call them to account. They do not attempt even to conceal their plunder. If everybody was not implicated in the robberies of the Treasury, some way would be found to bring them to light. All that people know is, that the State bonded debt has been increased from five to fifteen millions, and that, besides this, there are all sorts of current

2

obligations to pay afloat, issued by State officers who had authority to bind the Treasury. They are all tinctured with fraud, and some of them are such scandalous swindles that the courts have been able temporarily to stop their payment.

The whole of the late administration, which terminated its existence in November, 1872, was a morass of rottenness, and the present administration was born of the corruptions of that; but for the exhaustion of the State, there is no good reason to believe it would steal less than its predecessor. There seems to be no hope, therefore, that the villainies of the past will be speedily uncovered. The present Governor was Speaker of the last House, and he is credited with having issued during his term in office over $400,000 of pay "certificates" which are still unredeemed and for which there is no appropriation, but which must be saddled on the tax-payers sooner or later. The Blue Ridge Railroad scrip is another scandal embracing several millions of pure stealings. The case is briefly this: Some years ago a charter was obtained for a railroad across the southern end of the Blue Ridge from South Carolina into Kentucky. It was a difficult work, and the State promised it aid on certain conditions. The road was never made, and these conditions were never fulfilled, but since the restoration the State obligations were authorized to be issued. But this was

not the worst of it. The sum authorized was $1,-
800,000. It turns out that on the strength of this
authority over $5,000,000 of the scrip has been
issued. It was rendered available to the holders by
being made receivable for taxes, and in this way
has got spread abroad. The whole scheme has
been for the moment frustrated by a decision of
the courts that the entire transaction is fraudulent
and void from the start. With $5,000,000 of
this stuff afloat, which the Legislature can legalize
if the members are paid enough, what hope is
there that the State will escape liability for the
emission ?

These are sample items of the corruptions of
the late government outside of the increase of the
bonded debt. The iniquity laps over into this
administration, for the old Speaker has been
chosen Governor, and the present Legislature has
chosen Patterson Senator.

Yet the last canvass was carried on under the
sting of the charges of corruption against the
Scott administration, and it was hoped that the
present would be an improvement upon that. The
election of Patterson soon after the assembling of
the Legislature, and the manner in which he was
chosen, gave a sudden dash to those hopes. Then
it has been found that some of the most unscrupulous white and black robbers who have, as members or lobbyists, long plied their nefarious trade

at the capital, still disfigure and disgrace the present Assembly. So tainted is the atmosphere with corruption, so universally implicated is everybody about the government, of such a character are the ornaments of society at the capital, that there is no such thing as an influential local opinion to be brought against the scamps. They plunder, and glory in it. They steal, and defy you to prove it. The legalization of fraudulent scrip is regarded simply as a smart operation. The purchase of a senatorship is considered only a profitable trade. Those who make the most out of the operation are the best fellows. "How did you get your money?" was asked of a prominent legislator and lobbyist. "I stole it," was the prompt reply. The same man pursues his trade to-day, openly and unabashed. A leading member of the last administration was told he had the credit of having robbed the State of his large fortune. "Let them prove it," was his only answer. Meanwhile, both of them openly revel in their riches under the very shadow of the lean and hungry Treasury whence their ill-gotten gains were filched. As has been already said, it is believed that the lank impoverishment of the Treasury and the total abasement and destruction of the State credit alone prevent the continuance of robbery on the old scale. As it is, taxation is not in the least diminished, and nearly two millions per annum are raised for State expenses where $400,000 formerly sufficed. This affords succulent pasturage for a large crowd. For it must be remembered that not a dollar of it goes for interest on the State debt. The barter and sale of the offices in which the finances of the State are manipulated, which are divided among the numerous small counties under a system offering unusual facilities for the business, go on with as much activity as ever. The new Governor has the reputation of spending $30,000 or $40,000 a year on a salary of $3,500, but his financial operations are taken as a matter of course, and only referred to with a slight shrug of the shoulders.

Not only are the residences of the white thieves who have stolen their half a million or more apiece, pointed out in Columbia, but here and there a comfortable abode of some sable ally, whose sole business is politics. But while the colored brother has had to be content hitherto with smaller sums than the white, which of itself would account for want of relative show, he is also more prodigal in his expenditures. Still his savings are not to be despised. Sambo takes naturally to stealing, for he is used to it. It was his notorious weakness in slavery, and in his un-regenerate state he is far less culpable than the white. The only way he ever had to possess him-self of any thing, was to steal it from somebody else. The white man is really the responsible party for his thefts. He may well turn and say to his former master, "The villainy you teach, I will execute." The narration I have given sufficiently shows how things have gone and are going in this State, but its effect would be much heightened if there were time and room for details. Here is one: The total amount of the stationery bill of the House for the twenty years preceding 1861 averaged $400 per annum. Last year it was $16,000. But the meanness of these legislative robberies is not less significant of the character of the legislation than their magnitude. Last year the Treasury was in great straits on one or two occasions for money to anticipate the taxes. Some of the banks came to its aid and advanced about $60,000. They were this year compelled to go before the Committee of Claims to get reimbursed. The shameless rascals refused to pay the claim unless they were allowed to bag some 15 or 20 per cent. of it for their share! Another class of men who are allowed to rob the State freely, comprises those who control the printing-offices. The influence of a free press is well understood in South Carolina. It was understood and dreaded under the old *régime*, and was muzzled accordingly. Nearly all the newspapers in the State are now subsidized. The State government employs and pays them *ad libitum*. One installment of $75,000

lately went to about twenty-five papers in sums
ranging from $1,000 to $7,000 apiece, a list of
which was published by order of a vote of the
Legislature a short time ago. Down here these
small weekly sheets can be pretty nearly kept going on these subsidies. Of course, none of the
deviltry of the State government is likely to be
exposed through them. The whole amount of
the printing bills of the State last year, it is com-
puted (for every thing here has to be in part guess-
work), aggregated the immense sum of $600,000.

CHAPTER IV.

The Pure Blacks the Ruling Power.—Rivalries of Blacks and
Yellows.—Carpet-bag Rule wellnigh over.—The State gov-
erned by its own Citizens.

It is something more than a question of mere
curiosity, " Who rules this Legislature ? " It is,
to an overwhelming extent, as we have already
seen, composed of colored men. They are of
every hue, running from coal-black through all
the intermediate shades, out to what seems pure
white. There appears to be scarcely any limit
to the variety of shades of the colored population of the State, and their representatives in
the Legislature are hardly less various. There is
really no way of knowing whether any given individual in South Carolina has black blood in
his veins, except by tracing his descent. The
specimens of the whitened-out colored men in
the Legislature demonstrate this. But who leads
among this assembly of blacks and yellows ? Is
it the white men ? By no means ; Sambo has already outgrown that.

There is a strong disposition, among the old
whites of the State, to say and believe that it is

the white blood in the negro race which is managing affairs in the new *régime*. The pure blacks have been set so low in the scale, that it would show great want of penetration or great misrepresentation on the part of the old masters for them to admit the capacity of the black to conduct civic affairs, even as well as they are conducted here. Hence, all credit is apt to be denied them, and given to the element of white blood that courses in the veins of their lighter-colored brethren. Let us look about the Legislature and see how this is. The man who uniformly discharges his duties in the most unassuming manner and in the best taste, is the chaplain of the House. He is coal-black. In the dignities and proprieties of his office, in what he says, and, still better, in what he omits to say, he might be profitably studied as a model by the white political parsons who so often officiate in Congress. Take the chairman of the House Committee of Ways and Means. He is another full-black man. By his position, he has charge of the most important business of the House. He was selected for his solid qualities, and he seems always to conduct himself with discretion. Two of the best speakers in the House are quite black. Their abilities are about equal. Their moral qualities differ. One appears to be honest, and the other to be a rascal. They are both leaders rather than led.

Go into the Senate. It is not too much to say that the leading man of the Republican party in that body is Beverly Nash, a man wholly black. He is apparently consulted more and appealed to more, in the business of the body, than any man in it. It is admitted by his white opposition colleagues that he has more native ability than half the white men in the Senate. There is the Senator from Georgetown. He boasts of being a negro, and of having no fear of the white man in any respect. He evidently has no love for him. He is truculent and audacious, and has as much force and ability as any of the lighter-colored members of his race about him. He appears to be also one of the leading "strikers," and is not led, except through his interests. To say the least, none of the lighter-colored members of the race command any more consideration, or possess any more marked influence or talent, than these and other specimen blacks who might be named. So that there seems to be no reason for the conclusion that it is the white element in the negro race that is enabling this body of former slaves to discharge the functions of legislators. The full blacks are just as much entitled to the credit of what is done as the mulattoes.

The future results of this are yet to be developed in affairs here. History indicates that there is nearly as great an antagonism, when disputes

of race begin, between blacks and yellows as between blacks and whites. The germs of this antagonism already begin to show themselves here.
The white blood often takes on airs when it is
commingled as well as when it is unmingled.
The negro begins, as he did in Hayti, by getting
rid of the white man. After he is disposed of,
the mulatto may be pursued with equal persist-
ence. If South Carolina should be Africanized,
the same tendency to make it a pure black government would, it is likely, manifest itself here
as in Hayti. So far, however, the tendency has
only been to get rid of white local leaders; and,
as they have been hitherto mostly carpet-baggers,
there should be nobody to complain. It is such
a merit to drive them out, that nobody stops to
ask or care who follows them and fills their places.
Wherever those places have been filled by colored
men, the change has been advantageous to the
State. This is notably the case in the important
office of State Treasurer, who is a colored man
educated abroad by a rich father, who lived in
Charleston. But, as the Treasury of South Carolina has been so thoroughly gutted by the thieves
who have hitherto had possession of the State
government, there is nothing left to steal. The
note of any negro in the State is worth as much
on the market as a South Carolina bond. It
would puzzle even a Yankee carpet-bagger to

make any thing out of the office of State Treasurer under such circumstances.

Three of these old carpet-bag leaders, now out of place, remain in Columbia; each, it is said, rolling in wealth. They, with a few remaining greedy legislative comrades, whom Sambo has not yet dismissed, together with the present Governor, constitute the chief ornaments of that privileged society. Speaking generally, then, we may say that the State government of South Carolina is no longer in the hands of the carpetbaggers. It is in the possession of her own people. The present State officers, legislative and executive, are all, or nearly all, South Carolinians. The Governor is a South Carolina white man, the Lieutenant-Governor, the President of the Senate, the Speaker of the House, the Treasurer, and other State officers, are all of the sable tint, and all are alike natives. South Carolina has, therefore, to all intents and purposes, the charge of her own affairs. The evils she suffers from the character of her rulers grow out of the nature of the constituency which chooses them.

That the State has been victimized, plundered, and robbed by audacious scoundrels from abroad is not to be denied. But at home she is mainly rescued from their clutches, and it is not they whom the people of the State will have much longer to contend with. Those who would reform South Carolina in the future, will have chiefly its native population only to deal with. The black man of the Legislature feels his oats, and considers that the time has already arrived when he can take care of himself. He is not going to throw away, however, his party relationships, or his party advantages. He will use these in the future as he is now using them, to advance his own purposes. He is familiar with the uses of the caucus and the league, and he feels strongly the advantages of combination and concentration, and he has learned the trick of using them as well as his white brethren. It is sometimes said that, in these caucuses and leagues, all legislative affairs are shaped, and that here the white man bears sway. The action of the Legislature does not bear out this view. There was a measure up for consideration the other day in the House, in which the negroes broke away and voted alone. It was a bill for a railroad very much needed, and to which there could be and was no honest objection. But some of the corrupt negro leaders thought the corporation could be forced to pay for the charter, and if the members opposed it they could get pay for their votes. Accordingly, the great body of the blacks combined, and the bill was refused a passage by a decisive majority, who chuckled over their achievement as they would have done if they had cornered a rabbit in a cotton-field. The opposition was so evidently corrupt and scandalous, that not a single white man on either side in the body would allow himself to be caught in opposing the measure, and not one white vote was given against it. This is one instance among many to show that Sambo is fast getting out of leading-strings, and is already his own leader in the Legislature.

CHAPTER V.

A LARGE, well-built, showy kind of white man, with a good voice and fluent speech, was addressing the House yesterday. Standing beside me on the floor, near the Speaker's chair, was a snug-built, round-headed, young black man, of perhaps one-quarter white blood. He had full eyes, thick lips, and woolly hair, and was brusque and lively. I asked who was the speaker. "Oh," replied he, with a toss of the head and a scornful air, "that is a chuckle-head from ——. He has got about as much brains as you can hold in your hand." My pride of race was incontinently shocked. Here was a new view. It was no longer the white man deriding the incapacity of the negro. The tables were emphatically turned. It was Sambo proclaiming the white man's inferiority. Here, then, is something suggestive. "Soho! my friend," I said, "you know these people, then; give us your judgment of them."

He replied: "We have all sorts here, good,

bad, and indifferent." " Parsons among them ?"
"No, only a few. Not so many as formerly.
When I was on the stump at the last election, I
advised the people not to send the parsons. They
gave us a great deal of trouble. They had been
the most corrupt rascals we had in the Legislature. Now they are less plenty. We are improving. But see that darkey now talking. Isn't
it ridiculous that people should send such representatives They don't know any thing, and
haven't even decent manners. There is another
big fool, sitting there. Look at him. Why don't
they keep such chaps at home? They are a disgrace to the colored people." It was my snug-
built, thick-lipped, woolly-headed, small-brained,
black friend, you see, who was making these fruitful comments. The scene grew interesting. "How
about this Senator Patterson business?" "Well,
we sha'n't know any thing certain about it till it
is investigated. A member was boasting the
other day at a public table, before twenty fellow-
boarders and members, of his intentions. He
said that, where there was money going, a member was a fool who did not get his share. For his
part, he intended to make all he could. He was
here for that purpose. A while after Patterson's
election, this man was flush of money. He deposited $250 in bank, and displayed $150 more,
which he said he must reserve for current ex-

penses. Where he got his money nobody knows. All we know is this, that he had none when he came here." Then our colored friend added, with great *naïveté*, "Everybody is aware that the senatorial election is the only money measure that has been before the Legislature at this session."

"Who is this Whittemore, just elected by the Legislature as one of the trustees of the State Agricultural College?" "Oh, he is that white member of Congress who was turned out for selling his cadetship. He may do well enough for a place like that, but I should not vote for him if I had a seat here. I am a young man, just entered on a political career, and have a record to make, and I don't want to be mixed up with such fellows as Whittemore."

Here, again, we have virtuous Sambo on the corrupt white man. This is even more edifying. Whittemore is a white parson. Our friend is a black layman. We cordially sympathize in his youthful, praiseworthy resolutions. Who knows he will not hold to them steadfastly to the end? Let us hope. There is need he should. He bears one of the most honored names in South Carolina, and there is a good sprinkling of white blood in his veins. May he live long and illustrate the virtues of both races!

He continued: "You have heard of Beverly

Nash? There he sits. A full-blooded black man, six feet high. He is a good-looking man, with pleasing manners. He was formerly a slave of W. C. Preston, and afterward a bootblack at one of our hotels. He is now a substantial citizen, and a prominent leader in the Senate and in the State. He handles them all. The lawyers and the white chivalry, as they call themselves, have learned to let him alone. They know more of law and some other things than he does; but he studies them all up, and then comes down on them with a good story or an anecdote, and you better believe he carries the audience right along with him. All the laugh and all the ridicule is on his side. And when he undertakes a thing, he generally puts it through, I tell you. No, sir, there is now nobody who cares to attack Beverly Nash. They let him alone right smart."

"They were mostly slaves, these people in the Legislature?" "Yes, nearly all, including the Speaker of the House; not more than five or six were freeborn." "And you?" "No, sir, I never was a slave. I was raised in Charleston. My parents were free and my grandparents before them."

"You have United States troops in Columbia." "Yes, but we don't need them. The Kuklux did not bother anybody down here. We can take care of ourselves. Things are in rather a

bad fix in the State, financially, but they will all
come out right in the end. This town has suffered
greatly, but it is fast recovering. Sherman's
troops burnt the city. There is no doubt about
that. I myself lost a house, and I ought to be
paid for it; for if ever the sun shone on a loyal
man I am one. It cost $600 or $700, and could
not be rebuilt for twice the money. I am
sure I ought to be paid." It was evident our
bright belligerent black friend was not only bent
on a political "career," but also had a thrifty eye
to the main chance. But why not? Who shall
reproach him for that? "There were many black
mercenaries in the Legislature. Nobody could
dispute that. But the same thing existed elsewhere, didn't it, where things were whiter?" I
declined to contest that view of the case.

Turning to a solitary white man on my way
out of the crowd, he replied, to some remark, that
"to take the State of South Carolina away from
the intelligent white men and hand it over bodily
to ignorant negroes just escaped from slavery, because there happened to be four blacks to three
whites throughout the State, was nothing less
than flat burglary on the theory and practice of
representative government." I suggested, in reply, that the system of cumulative voting might
very much relieve the problem. If the whites
had their fair proportion of the representation,

say three to four, would not energy, talent, and
resolution, do the rest? But he was disinclined
to any hopeful view of the case. He said " the
darkey was not going to let up on any of the advantages he had. He was more inclined to be
aggressive than yielding. He was improving, but
he was already getting too big for his breeches.
Instead of giving the whites a show, he was rather
thinking of Africanizing the State. He felt he
could go alone. He was beginning to show the
cold shoulder to the white man. What did he
want of the white man? The white man put on
airs. He would not associate socially with the
colored brethren, neither would he introduce
them to his daughters. This thing could not last.
Genuine political equality means social equality
with the governing classes. If the white man
could not fraternize with them, then the white
man may go hang. Sambo will go it alone.
Why not? The white walking-stick will be dis-
pensed with. The white figure-head will be removed. Congo is sufficient unto itself. Every
thing was tending that way. It appeared like
ingratitude to their white emancipators, and perhaps this consideration would operate to retard
the movement. But look at the evidence. Here
were 101 Republicans in the Legislature. Out of
the whole number only seven were white men;
94 were colored. Did not this look like African-

izing things? In the executive government, to be sure, the Governor was white. He got his place by dancing at negro balls and speculating in negro delegates. But the Lieutenant-Governor was colored, and the President of the Senate, and the Speaker of the House, and the Treasurer of the State, and nearly all the rest of the officials. Here was Columbia. Half the population was white, but its Senator was colored, and its Representatives in the Legislature and in the city government were nearly all colored men. So were its policemen and its market-men. Everybody in office was a darkey. As for the white carpet-baggers, they were getting shoved out all round." My informant was undoubtedly well informed. He was more alive to the facts than another less interested might have been. For he was an office-holder and a carpet-bagger. His species have had their day in South Carolina. This he foresees, and naturally quakes in his shoes. His track in the State has been one of robbery and desolation, and there is none to lament his final expulsion, whoever follows.

CHAPTER VI.

The Raw Negro as a Legislator.—His Qualities and Qualifications.
—His Ignorance and Corruption.

THE highest style of legislative spoliation is as well understood in the South Carolina Legislature as in any Tammany conclave that ever existed. The whites were the original teachers, but the blacks have shown themselves to be great adepts as scholars. If any one will take the trouble to watch the votes of the colored Representatives in Congress from South Carolina, he will not have to come down into this State to see the fact illustrated. Messrs. Elliott and Rainey had no scruples about marching with the white thieving phalanx and voting double back pay to themselves.

We may be surprised at the imitative capacity of the negro in his new functions, and even at his occasional exhibition of sense and shrewdness. When we expect nothing it is a surprise to get something. In viewing him in his new relations it is, however, easy to fall into error both in underrating him and in overrating him.

No one will dispute the proposition that the rude and unlettered black man is no better than the raw and untrained white man, either morally or intellectually. It is not necessary to assume the old slave's inferiority to the ignorant white man to canvass his fitness as a legislator.

It is sometimes said he showed great magnanimity and forbearance in not cutting the throats of the masters' families when he was emancipated. His forbearance is a fact that is very generally recognized with gratitude throughout the South. Yet it must not be forgotten that he did not even then know if he himself was fairly out of prison. He has and had long been in the habit of feeling the presence of an iron authority over him, and he knew it still existed somewhere, when he saw his master flee and fall before it. Sambo is to have credit only for that salutary fear that restrains violence from apprehension of its consequences. It is not necessary nor just, however, to take away such credit as fairly belongs to him for his conduct in the great day of emancipation. But we must beware of being carried away by sentimental imaginings.

The ignorant, thievish, immoral, stupid, degraded black man, is then no better than the white man of the same description. The one is just as much of a barbarian as the other. The black savage is as degraded as the white savage.

If he has not been, while in slavery, as much of a criminal as the corresponding class in the old free States, it is because he has been under stricter surveillance and more rigid control.

While we concede the existence of much that is good and even intelligent in the dense masses of the black population of South Carolina, and thoroughly sympathize with its rejoicings over its happy issue from a cruel bondage, and its hopes of a better future, it is impossible not to recognize the immense proportion of ignorance and vice that permeates the mass. It is fearful to contemplate the thick-coming issues that result from emancipation and enfranchisement, which are now barely in the bud and in the blossom. The ignorance manifested is black with its denseness. And it is not too much too say that, as the negro, in slavery had absolutely no *morale*, he comes out of it entirely without *morale*. It is in the unpremeditated language of the leading Republican newspaper of Columbia, in advocating compulsory education, that the negroes are termed "ignorant, narrow-minded, vicious, worthless animals." This is the spontaneous criticism of an editor who is a child and a champion of black rule, betrayed accidentally into the expression of his real sentiments through the urgency of his advocacy of compulsory education. Yet the blacks where he lives are among the best in the State, and altogether more advanced in enlightenment than the inhabitants of the purely black counties in the lower part of the State.

With a constituency thus degraded, what are we to expect of its representatives?

The existing Legislature is already furnishing the answer. The black constituency of Charleston itself is to-day represented by men who belong in the penitentiary. The best that can be said is that the worst of these representatives are not black. But some of the lower counties have legislative specimens of black rascality that it would be hard to match in any white assembly.

The black men who led the colored forces the other day against a railroad charter, because their votes had not been purchased, were models of hardihood in legislative immorality. They were not so wily nor so expert, perhaps, as the one white man who was their ally in debate, but who dodged the vote from fear of his constituency; but they exhibited on that, as they have on other occasions, an entire want of moral tone, and a brazen effrontery in pursuing their venal purposes that could not be surpassed by the most accomplished "striker" of Tweed's old gang. I have before alluded to the fact that on this occasion the blacks voted alone, not one white man going with them in opposing the measure they had conspired to defeat in order to extort money from the corporators.

3

This mass of black representatives, however ignorant in other respects, were here seen to be well schooled in the arts of corruption. They knew precisely what they were about and just what they wanted, and they knew the same when they voted for Patterson for Senator.

This is the kind of moral education the ignorant blacks of the State are getting by being made legislators. The first lessons were, to be sure, given by whites from abroad. But the success of the carpet-baggers has stimulated the growth of knavish native demagogues, who bid fair to surpass their instructors. The imitative powers of the blacks and their destitution of *morale* put them already in the front ranks of the men who are robbing and disgracing the State, and cheating the gallows of its due.

It is bad enough to have the decency and intelligence and property of the State subjected to the domination of its ignorant black pauper multitude, but it becomes unendurable when to that ignorance the worst vices are superadded.

It was only a short time before the adjournment of the Legislature that the following occurrence took place: Some of the notorious plunderers had, a year or two before, obtained a charter to furnish the city of Charleston with pure water. They refused to execute the work, in order to extort a bonus from the city itself for the charter. The city declined to be robbed in this way, and went to the last Legislature for a new charter. Everybody was in favor of giving it except those interested in the old one. The knaves, by their boldness, were able to defeat the city and prevent the passage of its bill. This was accomplished in the Senate by a black man, who declared his purpose to defeat the measure by obstructive proceedings. The Senate was a unit for it, with the exception of three or four interested in the old charter, whom this sable legislator led. After a wearisome contest, in which all the arts of legislative obstruction were practised, this Senator finally moved an amendment providing for the introduction of hot water, and on this absurd proposition talked several hours in a night session, and threatened to talk all night. In this way the patience of the Senate was finally exhausted, and, with an overwhelming majority in favor of the measure, gave up the contest with the black fillibuster, and allowed him to defeat the bill. Who shall say, after this, that Sambo any longer needs carpet-baggers to lead him?

CHAPTER VII.

Humiliation of the White Minority.—Hostility of the Blacks to
Immigration.—Promise of the Future.

IN viewing the condition of South Carolina,
one naturally is led to inquire into the political
situation of its chief city, Charleston. An examination shows that the city is a mere cipher, with
neither representation nor influence in State affairs, and plays no part therein. The last remaining privilege of counting and recording its own
vote has been taken away from it by the last
Legislature, apparently for the reason that a majority of its citizens are opposed to the ruling
dynasty. That body has passed an act giving to
the Governor the appointment of commissioners
and sub-commissioners, who are to take entire
charge of the city elections, control the ballot-
boxes, count the votes, and of course manipulate
the electors in such way as they please. With
such wholly unscrupulous persons as they have
in Charleston to manage elections, this scheme is
equivalent to subverting the right of election altogether. Even under the present system, the con-

servative and property interests of the city have no representative in the Legislature. With its 50,000 inhabitants and $30,000,000 of taxable values, the city proper is literally unrepresented in the politics of the State. Its vote is merged in that of the county, which chooses all its Representatives on general ticket. The majority vote of the city is thus extinguished in the preponderating numbers of the swamp negroes for thirty miles around, who choose the city's representatives. It thus turns out that, of the whole eighteen members of the county, nearly all are negroes, and the few who are not are the lowest and worst sort of white men.

But, as if this injustice were not enough for Charleston to endure, the present Legislature has passed the act referred to, by which the city is to be robbed of the poor privilege of purifying her own ballot-box and counting her own votes !

The question often naturally arises, whether the two races cannot agree to a partnership rule. Philanthropy and patriotism unite in the earnest desire for such an experiment, but the character of the present dynasty destroys all chances for the trial of it. Natural jealousies, instead of being abated, as they might be, by honesty and fair play, are aggravated and widened by the conduct of the dominant power. Instead of there being any disposition to remedy the injustice that prevails, there is exhibited a purpose to aggravate it, as we see in the example before us. An incident has just occurred which, though not much in itself, also shows the drift of things: A good white Republican, serving, as postmaster at Charleston, to the satisfaction of everybody, has just been removed by the Federal Government at Washington, and a black man put in his place.

On this subject, William Cullen Bryant, a man as distinguished in the political as he is eminent in the literary world, and a stanch supporter of General Grant, thus speaks of the President: "We wish, for example, that he would turn out the person whom he has just appointed Postmaster of Charleston, and restore to office the man whom he unwisely, and contrary to the wish of the people of Charleston, removed."

With this disposition everywhere to crowd the white man and humiliate the minority, it is well-nigh impossible to initiate such reforms as the situation demands. One of the methods by which the minority have proposed to restore to themselves some power in the government of the State, is by adopting the system now prevailing in Illinois of minority representation, or cumulative voting; but, with the spirit that prevails in the State at present, this reform seems almost hopeless, and no echoes of the debates held in the Tax-payers' Convention on that question are any longer heard in the State.

And so in the matter of immigration. The material interests of the State clearly demand it. But the blacks are against it, as they fear its political consequences. A late debate in the Senate illustrated this. A bill was up to exempt new railroad enterprises and various enumerated kinds of manufactures from taxation. A black leader debated it, and in the course of his remarks took occasion to say he had heard, or overheard, a good deal from the class of people whom this legislation was designed to benefit; that it was intended to overslaugh and crowd out the blacks by foreign immigrants, to be introduced into the State by wholesale. Now, he wanted everybody to understand that the blacks did not intend to be crowded out, but that they proposed to stand their ground and "fight this thing out to the bitter end." He said they might bring on their immigrants, and they would find the blacks ready for them.

It was thus incidentally shown on that, as it often has been on other occasions, that the jealousy of the blacks is constant against the white man, and that they do not favor any influential participation by him in the government of the State. And, as in the case of Charleston, they are willing to perpetrate the greatest injustice to prevent it.

On the question of immigration, the present Governor is both for and against the measure. He knows the interest of the State requires it, and he knows his negro supporters are opposed to it. In his last annual message he thus declares himself in favor of immigration, but against immigrant foreigners. He admits the need of immigration in the abstract, but declares that the State wants no immigrants except from the Northern States. These he thinks would make excellent agriculturists. In a word, he is very eager in his invitations to a class of people whom he knows will not come, and turns his back upon and rebuffs those who would be glad to come.

This is all clear enough evidence as to the policy of the blacks and their corrupt white allies in regard to South Carolina. They desire to bind her down in her present degradation. Looking at the majorities they wield in the dense negro counties, they believe they can do it.

But, when we rise to a contemplation of those higher laws which govern the progress of humanity, we reach a belief that amounts to an assurance that Honesty and Intelligence will in the end be more than a match for Ignorance and Corruption; and that even South Carolina, reduced, beleaguered and prostrate as she is, will not always remain a prey to the influences which now rule the State. Looking at her situation and resources, and the invincible qualities that mark the Anglo-Saxon race, we cannot admit that she is going to be arrested in her progress, and least of all to recede and relapse into barbarism, because of her present abnormal condition. The State must burst its bonds. The energy of the American race, the nature of things, the demands of modern civilization, the pulsations of trade, commerce, public intelligence, and mechanic industry, throbbing through the intercourse by railroad and telegraph, and cooperating with the vital and pervading resources of the State, all seem to warrant the conclusion that a change must come. Although revolutions do not go backward, we feel that a state of things at once unequal and unnatural cannot endure. The whites must have in one way or another their relative weight in public affairs, not only in respect to the claim of numbers, but of the still weightier claims of property, intelligence, and enterprise. While the laws of the universe remain, these claims must in the end successfully assert themselves. Not even governments can prevent it. And it is about time for the Federal Administration to take this reflection to heart.

CHAPTER VIII.

The Rule of the Negro in South Carolina.—What it is, what it portends.—Education.

The rule of South Carolina should not be dignified with the name of government. It is the installation of a huge system of brigandage. The men who have had it in control, and who now have it in control, are the picked villains of the community. They are the highwaymen of the State. They are professional legislative robbers. They are men who have studied and practised the art of legalized theft. They are in no sense different from, or better than, the men who fill the prisons and penitentiaries of the world. They are, in fact, of precisely that class, only more daring and audacious. They pick your pockets by law. They rob the poor and the rich alike, by law. They confiscate your estate by law. They do none of these things even under the tyrant's plea of the public good or the public necessity. They do all simply to enrich themselves personally. The sole, base object is, to gorge the individual with public plunder. Having done it, they turn

around and buy immunity for their acts by sharing their gains with the ignorant, pauperized, be-
sotted crowd who have chosen them to the sta-
tions they fill, and which enable them thus to
rob and plunder.

Are we to be told that these things are inevitable because they are the results of our theory
of government, and that that theory must be
sound? Is not the true reasoning quite in the
other direction? If these are the legitimate results of it,. then the theory is at fault, and its
application must somehow be changed or modified. What the world is after is results—sound,
wholesome, just results. These every intelligent
and resolute community will have, sooner or later,
in one way or another. They will not forever
endure tyrannies, and oppressions, and outrages.
It is the corruptions and the abuses of authority
that stimulate revolutions, rupture kingdoms, and
overturn empires. This is as true now and will
be as true in the future as it has been in the past.
Fraud, injustice, misrule in government, whatever their protean shapes, whether lofty or low,
whether noble or ignoble in their aspects, will
breed a temper that will seek to accomplish their
overthrow. Especially must this be so in our
times. Does anybody suppose that such a condition of things as exists to-day in South Carolina
is to last? Such a supposition is to ignore the his-

tory and the character of mankind. Suppose the men, or a large portion of the white men, of South Carolina who have gone through the War of the Rebellion are cowed and demoralized by its results ; how is it with the individuals of the rising generation who are fast taking their places? Is not the hot blood of the South in their veins ? They have the ardor of youth. They have the stimulus of young ambition ; they have the pride of ancestry ; they have the inherited valor of successive generations. Have they no part to play in the future ? We may rest assured that no depressing circumstances of the present are going to destroy or repress the natural development that comes of race and of blood. Opportunity alone is wanting ; and that, we know, is always found by the bold and aspiring.

In pointing to these dangers, which the future has in store, we take the same conservative part that we did in warning the Northern Democracy and the rabid slave-holder against the daring attempt to force slavery into the Free Territories. We then pleaded for the rights of freemen and the demand of justice. We do the same now. We opposed oppression then, we oppose oppression now. The circumstances are different, the elements of the case are different, but the fundamental principle underlying the action then and the action now is identical. It is the true function of conservatism in government to recognize present and to foresee future danger and guard against it. It was true conservatism to expose the evils of slavery and aim to prevent its spread. It is true conservatism now to expose the frightful results of the rule of ignorance, barbarism, and vice, and to visit with unsparing condemnation a condition of affairs as perilous and as threatening to the future peace and prosperity of the country as any that ever preceded it in our history.

Those who suppose that any thing short of a good government in the State of South Carolina, and, we may add, of any other State similarly situated in the South, is going to long stand, or be tolerated, may well take heed, if their judgments are ever to find expression in action. The history of Hungary is before us. The history of Poland is before us. The history of Ireland is before us. Where there is actual injustice, or radical wrong in the government, it breeds resistance. That wrong may be even in part sentimental. It is none the less real for that. The present government of South Carolina is not only corrupt and oppressive, it is insulting. It denies the exercise of the rights of white communities, because they are white. The city of Charleston is an example, as we have heretofore shown. The black government of the State denies it the right to superintend its own voting, or to count its own votes.

There is always a calm after a rebellion is
quelled.   There is always a time when "order
reigns in Warsaw."   But, unless justice is established, a storm follows.   The revolutionary spirit
is a catching disorder.   It is even more—it is
hereditary.   In these later times wise rulers have
been taught a lesson.   They have learned to
remove just causes of complaint.   We are just
having our first trials in this line reach the ear of
the Federal Government.   They already come in
trumpet-tones from at least two States in the
Union.   Have the men who are in temporary
charge of our national affairs the ability, the
skill, or the perception of the situation that is
requisite to deal with them?

These remarks are not intended to perpetuate
discontent or hostility.   They are plain, frank
words, addressed to the good sense and the intelligence of the reader.   They speak to the judgment only.   If they have any force, it comes of
their truth and justice alone.   They are but an
exposition and a warning.   They have no object
beyond that of attracting public attention to existing scenes, circumstances, and events that are
alike full of interest and full of peril to the country.

The question is often asked if education is not
the remedy for the blackness of darkness that
prevails in South Carolina.   Yes, indeed, if that
were possible.   Make it compulsory then.   But

what is education? Is it the glib recitation of
the alphabet, or the multiplication-table? Is it
the knowledge of reading and writing? This is
all that compulsory education can give, in its
most successful forms. But here is a race to be
educated in the very elements of manhood. They
have to be taught positively and negatively. The
education they require is the formation of a race
the opposite of the existing race. They have to
be taught not to lie, not to steal, not to be un-
chaste. To educate them properly is to revolu-
tionize their whole moral nature. The ground-
work of that education which will make them fit
rulers of a republic will not even have been laid
when they shall be taught reading and writing.
It is the reading and writing negroes of the South
Carolina Legislature who lead in its most infamous
venalities and corruptions. This sort of education
merely lends a cutting edge to their moral obtuse-
ness. Education, to be what it ought to be with
the existing race of negroes in the South, means
to educate them out of themselves, means to undo
the habits and practices and modes of thought
and want of thought engendered by centuries of
slavery. It means the moral enlightenment and
regeneration of a whole people debauched and
imbruted for ages. Such is the gigantic task demanded of an education suited to existing circumstances.

We do not mean to say that all this is necessary to entitle the colored man to the privileges of citizenship, but only mean it as a reply to the glib suggestion of compulsory education as a ready remedy for the existing disorders and crimes that disgrace republican government and menace its future. Neither is it any answer to say that other people are ignorant, and superstitious, and degraded. When the ignorant and superstitious and degraded subjects of other nationalities have shown themselves capable of governing the better classes of society, it will be time to plead their example and their qualifications for the functions of rulers. But they are the classes who have never yet in history exercised the functions of government. And thus the fact that they exist from age to age, and that their presence does not destroy governments, proves nothing. They have lived as pupils in the State, and not as its masters, as they now live in South Carolina. Let us not be misunderstood. We are not talking about denying rights of citizenship. We are denouncing governments of ignorance and vice, and demanding a remedy.

Again, there is no parallel to be drawn between the exceptional venality of Northern Legislatures and the corruptions of South Carolina government. They do not spring from the same causes. The former can be promptly remedied by ex-

posure and by an appeal to the intelligence and
virtue of the constituency; in the other case there
is no such tribunal to appeal to. It is a moral
morass in which there is neither standing nor
holding ground.

CHAPTER IX.

The Character of the Negro, morally and intellectually.

SOUTHERN thinking minds have always been deeply exercised over the problem of the black population, from Mr. Jefferson down. They strive to master it. They try hard to elucidate it. They have an unconquerable desire to find holding-ground for their speculations. They look backward, and around them, and forward to the future, to try and discover a philosophy and a theory which shall explain the various and curious facts brought to their knowledge, and guide them out of the smoky labyrinth wherein they grope. But that full solution they so much desire always eludes their grasp. Africa rises always to their view. There the negro has had sway through unnumbered centuries. There he is a barbarian still. Give him sway elsewhere, will his condition be different? What ground is there for the supposition? When the white element exists in him, it modifies but does not improve him.

It is the uniform testimony of experience and observation that the pure black is the best man. The admixture of white blood does no good, but the contrary. The half-breed is more treacherous, more passionate, more vicious, more delicate in constitution. But the black is a child of vice and ignorance and superstition in South Carolina as well as in Africa. What he might have been capable of, under different conditions than those in which he has ever existed, it is useless to inquire. Races of men exhibit the same general characteristics from age to age. The question which concerns us is, not what might be, or what in some remote future may be, but what now is. The negro is suddenly thrust into conspicuous prominence in our political system, and it is his present condition, qualities, habits, propensities, that we have to deal with, and we are now all alike deeply interested with his former masters in considering the problem of his character. He is certainly not the kind of man, and his race is not the race, for whom our political institutions were originally made ; and it is already a serious question whether he is the man, or his the race, for which they are adapted. We have but barely entered upon the experience which is to furnish a solution of this question. It is one we need to study and try to master. The overshadowing mass of black barbarism at the South hangs like a portentous cloud upon the horizon. The country boldly confronted the question of slavery and as boldly destroyed it. It is gone, and gone forever. No man wishes to restore it. Not even in South Carolina is that man to be found. The best thinkers of the South to-day tell us they bless God for the war. It was necessary to get rid of slavery. But for slavery, they believe, the original slave States of the South would be among the greatest and most flourishing of all our commonwealths. It is the negro who has been the innocent cause of their despoliation. It is the negro that rests like an incubus upon them. Their vital forces pulsate under ribs of iron which will not give them play. It is the man from Africa who to-day bestrides them like a colossus. He came in helplessness, he has risen in strength. He was the servant of South Carolina; he has become her master.

These are the appalling facts that make it important and necessary that the negro should be studied and understood by the whole country. It is not a question for South Carolina merely; it is a question for the nation. For it is a question of the predominance and antagonism of races. If it be true that this is not a white man's government, is it true of any State that it shall be a black man's government? It is a question for statesmanship to answer whether it can be expected that the white man will long stand pas-

sively by and see all the power of legislation
wielded by the inferior race. And more: whether
he can be expected to witness patiently the still
more exasperating spectacle of the ignorance and
venality of the blacks, bearing sway over the intelligence, probity, and honest manhood of the
State. There is a moral element in every State.
There is its conscience, its sense of right, its ha-
tred of wrong. These are its genuine and unconquerable revolutionary forces. Once roused, and
we have a State on fire, and a fire which politics
and politicians are always powerless to quench.
It is the fanaticism of justice, which the stars in
their courses sustain, and against which no attri-
bute of the Almighty takes part.

We only disposed of one phase of the negro
question in abolishing slavery. The great per-
plexity of establishing just relations between the
races in the negro States is yet to be encountered.
And it comes upon the country under a cloud of
embarrassments. It has to be settled under the
growing urgency and doubtful solution of the question whether the great mass of the black population at the South is not now mentally and morally
unfit for self-government, and whether the progress of events will not force a modification of the
original reconstruction acts—not based upon race
or color or previous condition, but upon other
considerations yet to be evolved and elucidated.

Fancy the moral condition of a State in which a large majority of all its voting citizens are habitually guilty of thieving and of concubinage. Yet such is the condition of South Carolina. Are we to be told that the civilization of the nineteenth century has nothing better to propose than this for the government of one of the oldest and proudest States of the American Union?

As it is morally, so it is intellectually. These same rulers of a great State, speaking of them as a whole, neither read nor write. They are as ignorant and as irresponsible in the exercise of their political functions as would be the Bedouin Arab of the desert, or the roving Comanches of the plains, if called upon to choose the rulers of New York or Massachusetts. Is this the self-government for which a war of seven years was waged, in which the best blood of a nation was shed, and to secure the results of which a written Constitution was painfully elaborated by its wisest and most conscientious men, in order that justice and liberty might forever be maintained in the States of the model American Republic? Tell us what government of any civilized state of the Old World, if imported into South Carolina, would be as oppressive upon, and as unfitted for, the 300,-000 white people of that State, as that which now curses it under the name of republican!

CHAPTER X.

The South as it is, and not as it seems.—The Demands of Justice and Statesmanship.

It was not the whole Southern people that were fools or criminals, in the matter of secession, by any means. It was really but a handful of leaders, not one of whom was of sound mind, that precipitated the insane attempt to take the slave-holding States out of the Union. But for half a dozen men, who never made any figure in the real work of the rebellion afterward, there would have been no secession and no war. It was Toombs, and Slidell, and Rhett, and Mason, and Jeff Davis, who were the malignant spirits of the contest, and without whom the war would not have been made. The men who commanded the Southern armies, like Lee and the Johnstons, and Stonewall Jackson, and Longstreet; and the more eminent of the civilians who carried on the rebel government, as R. M. T. Hunter, Alexander H. Stephens, and Benjamin, would never have moved hand or foot to initiate secession. They, and even such men as Governor Wise, were hurried along by a popular current, set in motion by the radicals of the slave-holding party, which they found themselves powerless to resist. Wise was one of the most fiery of the slave-holders, but even he was against secession. There was thus no unanimity even among the dominant party of the South, who had acquired ascendency from their loud protestation of their peculiar devotion to the interests of the South, and signalized it repeatedly in Congress by their furious denunciations of everybody who would not worship the offensive god of their own idolatry. Much of what they said and did was purely dramatic and designed to advance personal and political ends. They played the part of the demagogue with the objects of the demagogue, and with no serious intention of rupturing the Union, or bringing on a bloody war. We say, without fear of contradiction, that, during the ten years that preceded the breaking out of the rebellion, not one in ten of the members from the slave States favored disunion in any event. The inflammatory speeches in behalf of slavery, and against those who opposed its spread, were generally made by those engaged in a race for popular favor at home. They were for bunkum. And some of the most distinguished of the surviving actors in those efforts have to-day no hesitation in avowing it. The only excuse for their criminality is to be found in their ignorance of

the mischief they were committing. They helped
to fill the magazine with materials, which a few
others, more bold and more reckless, exploded.
They helped to " fire the Southern heart," and to
popularize the sentiment that to oppose the exten-
sion of slavery into territory where it did not exist,
was in some way an aggression upon Southern
rights, which ought to be resisted. This sentiment was spread by these dramatic and dema-
gogical efforts, and enabled the handful of secession leaders to excite the sudden ebullition of
popular fervor, which finally carried the secession
conventions without any majority behind them.

Outside the ranks of the slave-holders themselves, whose own divisions were such as we have
depicted, there was a vast body of moderate, conservative men, who had no part or lot in agitating
the slavery question. They were men who, finding slavery as a birthright and an inheritance,
aimed to make the best of their situation. They
deprecated agitation, and desired to remove it
from the field of political discussion. They held
to no extremes of opinion either in regard to its
spread or its abolition. They were beset by no
mad conceits of a slave empire, and their moral
sense had not been so corrupted that they desired
its unending perpetuation. They viewed slavery
as an evil, but an evil to be endured, till a way,
yet unseen by them, was opened for its extinction.

4

They saw it was a question of an inflammable character, easily made the stepping-stone of ambition, and requiring constant efforts to allay strife and contention in regard to it. These they patriotically and devotedly made, opposing rampant abolitionism on the one hand, and slave-mongering and slave-spreading on the other. A vast proportion of substantial citizens of the South were of this way of thinking always. It was this class who kept many of the best men of the South in Congress as their representatives, for long years, and who went under at last, as the banks of a river go under during a destructive rise of its waters. That body of men in the South were submerged by the rebellion, but they were not converted and not wholly destroyed. They and their descendants exist to-day, a large, growing, powerful, upright phalanx of worthy citizens. They are the men, and the descendants of men, who sent such representatives to Congress as John Bell, of Tennessee, and Berrien, of Georgia, and Governor Aiken, Edward Stanley, and Willie P. Mangum, of the Carolinas, and a host of others of kindred virtues and talents, whose wisdom and moderation were the pride of the nation.

There is another view of the case that should not be overlooked. Notwithstanding the vigor with which the rebellion was sustained by the Confederate troops in the field, there is abundant testimony to show that, after the first sudden voluntary rush to arms which marked the opening of the contest, the heart of the people was never in the war. The idea had been sedulously inculcated that it was to be a mere holiday affair. Ex-Senator Chesnut, of South Carolina, proclaimed in the secession convention of that State, that he would drink all the blood that would be shed in consequence of secession. But, when it was found that earnest war was to be the result, the mass of the people were wholly averse to remaining in the army. As fast as their first short terms expired they hastened to return to their homes, and they never left them except as they were dragged out by the strong arm of military power. It was only by exercising despotic authority, and by being utterly callous and conscienceless in its exercise, that the Confederate authorities recruited the rebel armies. And, notwithstanding all the exertion made, the losses by desertion were so great at times as to threaten the absolute dissolution of the army. In one of the incautious speeches in which President Davis indulged himself in a tour through South Carolina during the war, he substantially admitted this. The testimony now is uniform in the South that, as the war progressed, the troops made use of every excuse and opportunity to flee from the ranks and go to their starving households. A little handful of self-styled chivalry clung to the Confederate standard, urged thereto by the stimulants of personal pride and female pique, which urged them on, but these sentiments and influences had no weight with the mass.

It is only on this theory that we can account for the sudden and, at the time, almost inexplicable collapse of the Southern armies after Lee was driven from Richmond. They disappeared like the mist under the morning sun, while friends and allies both in this country and Europe were confidently predicting a fresh and strenuous guerrilla resistance in detail.

Little did those allies know of the sufferings the rank and file had endured in fighting battles in which they had no interest, or how they had skulked, deserted, hid, and been hunted by bloodhounds, and torn from their suffering families under the most heartless and cruel circumstances. Thus oppressed, they only too willingly threw away their arms and returned to the welcome avocations of peace. They were men without a grievance or a complaint. They had never been oppressed, and they knew it. They had never been denied a personal nor a political right enjoyed by the most favored citizen of the republic. Why should they voluntarily continue a war against such a Government? The answer was found in their subsequent action. They never did. They never raised a hand to prolong the contest a day. This striking fact is the testimony of the rank and file in regard to the character of the wrongs the Confederate Government were professedly attempting to right.

We think there is full justification for the statement that a vast majority of the Southern people were entrapped by a handful of ambitious leaders, destitute of the first elements of sound statesmanship, into a war for which there was no provocation, and which they would never have deliberately confronted. But, war once begun, they were in a vise. A despotic military government was thenceforth their master. To that is to be imputed all that followed.

Considerations like these may lead us to inquire whether the South of our imagination, as seen through the smoke and the blood and the fire of civil war, is not something very different from the real South that was dragged into secession, or the actual South of to-day.

The war, the events of the war, the men of the war, hang like a thick, impenetrable curtain before the eyes of the present generation of Northern people, hiding from view a past history, and existing facts, and a present situation, all of which are profoundly essential to a proper understanding of the problem with which the statesmanship of the country has now to deal. There is in the

South to-day an enormous mass of inherited worth, and virtue, and capacity, and wisdom, and every solid element of citizenship, that has an indefeasible right to demand recognition, and justice, and fraternal consideration. The commonest sentiments of humanity require it. The ties of a common lineage and a common government demand it. It is no more than we extend to the most worthless specimens of humanity of foreign birth that are annually landing upon our shores. Every generous impulse prompts it. The dictates of a wise statesmanship imperiously exact it. Nothing stands in the way of such recognition, but a blind, selfish, partisan hostility, that is as undying in its revenges as it is merciless in its judgments.

It is necessary to awake to the necessity of exterminating this hateful obstacle. It is time prejudice and enmity were put aside. In an eager desire to secure the natural rights of one set of people, we have quite overlooked the claims of another. In carelessness of the sufferings of the guilty, the heavy hand of injustice has been laid upon the innocent.

CHAPTER XI.

United States Troops in Carolina.—Destruction of the South Carolina University.—A Bastard Government.—Reform demanded.

AMONG the significant peculiarities to be observed in Columbia is the presence of United
States troops. They occupy barracks on the outskirts of the town, in a pleasant quarter, where
they drill daily, where the flag always floats, and
where military music is heard at sunset. Among
the airs often played is that which refers to the
late John Brown, of Ossawattomie. The gentle
reminder contained in that piece of music seems
to be particularly superfluous during the sessions
of the present South Carolina Legislature. For
if any thing would demonstrate the fact that the
soul of that immortal person is marching on, it
would be the living presence of that body of legislators. But the music seems to create no ripple
of discontent. It is a favorite pastime of the
"Gig Society" of Columbia to drive every evening to the parade-grounds and listen to such
strains as the band chooses to discourse. Out of
the multitude no one runs away at the sound of

John Brown's name. The military have no ter-
rors for this community, and their presence is
welcomed rather than deprecated. They are not
regarded in the light of an offensive symbol of
authority; the money they spend and the music
they make are considered a good deal more than
an offset for any sentimental objections that it
might be fancied their presence would excite.

Near by the parade-grounds are the college
buildings of the University of South Carolina.
Before the war their walls sheltered some two
hundred students. Their young blood was fired
by the first tap of the drum, and they all rushed
to the field. They have not come back. What
was to be a pastime proved a stern reality. The
buildings look worn and desolate, and only a handful of scholars and a few poorly-paid professors
remain. In execution of the steady purpose of
putting the blacks on an equality with the whites,
a measure was passed at this session to throw
open the library to the colored students of the
Normal School, and to take one of the college
buildings for its uses. And in pursuance of the
same purpose a majority of the trustees of the college were recently chosen by the same Legislature from the ranks of the blacks. In this case
it was color rather than qualification for the post
that was sought. This destroys the usefulness of
the college so far as the white youth are con-

cerned, as the young aristocratic blood of the
State will decline the proposed amalgamation.
The movement will eventuate in the substantial
destruction of the university, as the black population will afford an inadequate supply of students.   It is a damaging blow to the interests of
education in the State, and a significant step in
the process of Africanization.   But, even if the
college could be allowed to remain in the hands
of the whites, such is their stripped condition that
it would be difficult to maintain its former prosperity.   Still, it would have afforded to the youth
of the State a sort of domestic intellectual holding-
ground, of great service during the present transition stage.   Its capture by the blacks is a useless humiliation to the whites, since its advantages will now be lost to both races.   It does great
evil and it does no good.   It is an attack upon the
prejudices of the whites from no other motive than
desire of domination.   Rather than relinquish the
opportunity to control the college, the blacks are
willing to destroy it.   The class of whites that
support institutions of learning naturally decline
enforced intellectual association with the new
masters of South Carolina, and we judge will not
be accounted particularly fastidious for this pecu-
liarity.

In whatever direction we turn our eyes, we
find such details of the operation of this anoma-

lous government confronting us that we are provoked to speculations and comparisons impossible to repress. We know that changes of government often shove one set of men from their stools
in order that their seats may be occupied by ri-
vals. Thus the Huguenots, after Henry IV. of
France ; thus the Stuarts of England ; thus the
elder and the later Bourbons of St.-Germain,
were overthrown. The philosophical student of
history sympathizes comparatively little with the
lamentations over such and like mutations. The
successful and the vanquished stand upon the
same general plane of equality. At the worst, it
is but hereditary rank giving way to plebeian
energy and intellect. It is no worse than the
genuine force of Nature in any instance, that
conquers and assumes control. But it does this
by virtue of its own intrinsic power. It does it
through the God-given prerogative of capacity
and strength of character. Above all, it does it
of its own motion, and by dint of its own exertion. And when the result is accomplished, civilization has received no backward set. In all
modern history there has been no substitution of
ignorance for knowledge, of barbarism for cultivation, of stolidity for intelligence, of incapacity
for skill, of vice and corruption for probity and
virtue, in the revolutions and changes that have
taken place. The transitions, however trying to

individuals and dynasties, have been on the same
general plane of equality to the eye of history,
have been in the general interest of civilization,
and they do not startle us by offensive or shocking peculiarities or degradations. But it is altogether otherwise in the case of South Carolina.
Here is one to which all modern history does not
furnish a parallel. The changes here experienced have been accomplished by outside forces.
The result has not been produced by a wrestle
between two powers, in which the stronger has
thrown and taken the place of the weaker. The
strong has put the weak under foot, but has with-
drawn itself after placing upon the neck of its
prostrate foe the yoke of an ignoble and an incompetent crowd. They reign and rule by virtue of no merit, no intelligence, no prowess, no
capacity of their own, but by means of an alien
and borrowed authority only. Obedience is enforced by a power foreign to the instrument that
inflicts the humiliation. It is not the rule of intrinsic strength; it is the compulsive power of
the Federal authority at Washington. But for
that, the forces of civilization would readjust
themselves and overturn the present artificial
arrangement.

The State really bears a foreign yoke; not
one imposed by its own people, or by an authority which has arisen of itself among themselves.

And this is the anomaly of the situation. It is a so-called democracy sustained by external force. In other words, it is a government that the intelligent public opinion of the State would overthrow if left to itself. It may be called self-government, or republican or democratic government, but in no just sense is it either. It is a government which in the very nature of things could never rise to control, of itself, in any community. It is not an outgrowth of power and authority in the regular order. It is a hybrid born of unnatural connections, offensive alike to God and man ; and, wherever the retributive responsibility of it fairly belongs, it is clear that it does not belong to the generation now rising upon the stage of action in the South, and who alone will be in the near future the sole victims of its oppressions. And this is the class whose just rights must be considered, whose hardships must be mitigated and removed by the power which holds the actual control of the situation, or another and yet another political and social convulsion will inevitably ensue, till disorder and revolution become chronic in our affairs. Not till absolute justice is established can we look for peace and tranquillity in our political system anywhere.

CHAPTER XII.

THE Federal Government could do much, if it would take the necessary pains, toward correcting some of the worst practices of this corrupt travesty of a government. It did something in the appointment of Governor Orr as minister to Russia. It was at least an expression of sympathy with those who made an effort at reform at the last election. But it accomplished nothing of real value. In fact, by sending a leading supporter of the Administration, who was an opponent of corruption, 5,000 miles out of the country, it took away an influence which might, on occasion, deter the rogues from some of their more nefarious acts.

The only authority to which these miscreants pay the least deference is the Federal Government; for its power and its countenance are requisite to the success of many of their own operations. It makes large appropriations for new public edifices in the State, as is attested by those which are now going up in Charleston and Columbia. It appoints to office the large body of revenue officers, both internal and external, the numerous postmasters, the Federal judges, attorneys, and special agents, and it keeps bodies of Federal troops in the State, which are everywhere welcome for the money they disburse. Through these and kindred influences, the Federal Government holds vast sway over the State. That for some reason it has not exercised its influence to any appreciable extent in the interest of good government, is evident. It might do much toward repressing many corrupt practices and raising the moral tone of the State government. It has not done this. And yet it would seem to be its interest to do it. Why should the Republican party of the country, composed so largely as it is of its best and most conscientious citizens, be compelled to endure the foul stain inflicted by the robberies and outrages of caitiffs, who deserve the State-prison? Some of the leaders of affairs are men who have merely adopted Republicanism as a cloak for their villainies. South Carolina to-day rejoices in a Republican Representative in Congress who once made a formal proposition in the State Legislature to reduce all the free blacks to slavery, and it has a republican Governor who tore down the American flag from Fort Sumter, and, treading it under foot, hoisted the Confederate ensign

in its place. Dancing at negro balls and issuing
" pay certificates " as Speaker is said to have been
the means whereby he has condoned his offenses.
One turns with inexpressible loathing and disgust
from such wretched demagogues. They cover
Republicanism with reproach, and, what is worse,
they depress and extinguish the hopes of philanthropic men who wish to see the capacity and
better qualities of the black man fairly tested in
the bold experiment of his sudden emancipation
and enfranchisement.

It is of no service to the colored man or his
cause to disguise the exact facts of the situation,
or to paint things otherwise than as they are. If
what is now failure could have been made even a
partial success through faithful effort and honest
endeavor, what denunciation is too severe and
what punishment too great for those who have
disgraced a cause, and imperiled if not sacrificed
it by their unscrupulous greed? These dusky
children of the Legislature greet with a loving
embrace the reports of congressional corruption,
of the practices of the various criminals whose
hidden deeds have been brought to light by the
recent investigations. The bribed and thrice-
bought negroes roll these reports as sweet morsels
under their tongues. It is one of the worst feat-
ures of these great corruptions at the centre that
they strengthen, increase, and keep in counte-

nance those of the outskirts. Their reflective action is even more mischievous than their direct
consequences. The crimes of high places are used
to excuse and justify those of remoter regions.
Pollution at the centre becomes the source of a
thousand infectious streams flowing in every
direction toward the circumference. It discour-
ages the criticism and cripples the influence of
the honest indignation of the country, when it
can no longer lean upon a solid body of honesty
and probity among the chosen few who publicly
represent the nation. One known public dishonesty in Washington is the parent of a hundred in South Carolina. The external aids to
this State to enable her to extricate herself from
the Slough of Despond in which she is at present
stalled, it is thus readily seen, are much weakened
by the condition of things outside. The Federal
Government may plead it has its hands full nearer
home. Nevertheless, as we began by saying, it
ought to do, and it might do, a great deal for the
State, if it would. If it would drive partisan
politics into the sea, and undertake to administer
Federal affairs here strictly on the basis of honesty
and integrity, it might at least begin a break-
water to the general torrent of corruption that
pervades the State.

But the whites must rely mainly upon themselves, and mainly upon action quite outside and

independent of politics, to redeem the State, if it
is to be redeemed. This is the real serious work
they should set about. The old historic and really
important city of Charleston, with its fifty thousand inhabitants and thirty millions of taxable
values, is not to be lightly surrendered, however
threatened. It is the same with the various other
towns of less consequence, but still of importance,
throughout the State. Then the extraordinary
magnitude of its agricultural and other resources,
always great, and capable of still further development, is a living and standing protest against a
pusillanimous yielding to adverse circumstances.
It would be a violent presumption against the
manliness, the courage, and the energy of South
Carolina white men, to allow the State to remain
in the permanent keeping of her present rulers.
It would be a testimony against the claims of
Anglo-Saxon blood, and it would be an emphatic
testimony to the decline of public virtue that
would be worse than all. These considerations
alone should be sufficient to inspire every white
man in South Carolina with a resolution to achieve
a reform that will bring the State back to its an-
cient respectability. The feeling that most op-
presses the whites, arises from the great apparent
majority of colored voters as shown in the elections. This majority is reckoned to be about
30,000. But this arises from the fact that all the

blacks vote, while the whites do not. There is
no such majority as appears on the record, as the
relative black and white population by the census
clearly shows. The blacks are 400,000, the whites
are over 300,000. The actual majority, then, cannot be over 20,000.

But a comparison of the population of 1860
with that of 1870 shows some encouraging feat-
ures. The black population of the State during
that decade, though they did not enter the army,
increased but by the small number of 3,500;
while the whites, who were all in arms during
the war, and who lost 12,000 fighting men, besides
the loss of increase thereby entailed, managed to
hold their own within the trifle of about 1,600.
On the basis of the general law of population the
expectation is encouraging. But the period might
be greatly shortened by powerful and concen-
trated effort to the same end. The fact of the
State being so completely in possession of the
blacks, it is supposed, will and does attract the
colored people of other States. But the black
population is everywhere poor and immobile, and
though there is a movement toward the towns, it
does not appear in the agricultural districts. In
these there are blacks enough. The class there
wanted is of immigrants who have a little money,
and who buy land, and farm on their own account.
And such do come, and will be more and more

encouraged to come. It is their thrift and their energy and their money that are going to play an important part in overcoming the predominance of the black population. Where the white man can live and prosper, and enjoy good health, as he can all over the upper country or bluff-lands of South Carolina, he is bound to supplant the weaker and poorer race. So that the restoration of the predominance of the white population in the State seems to be only a question of time, which can be much abbreviated by suitable effort.

CHAPTER XIII.

Immigration its Greatest Need.—A Naked and Desolate State.—
Prejudices against White Immigrants still existing.—Greater
Political Tolerance demanded.

THE experience of South Carolina during and
since the war is one of the most tragic episodes
in history. When before did mankind behold
the spectacle of a rich, high-spirited, cultivated,
self-governed people suddenly cast down, bereft
of their possessions, and put under the feet of the
slaves they had held in bondage for centuries?
It was a severe blow to the people of South
Carolina to have their slaves emancipated without compensation. It was as great a shock as
society is often called to endure, to have the masters and their families, brought up in luxury and
idleness, suddenly thrown back upon themselves,
and compelled in suffering and destitution to get
on as they best might, without aptitude and
without experience.

They lost every thing they possessed in the
shape of property, except the soil of the State
and the buildings thereon spared from the deso-

lation of war. The banks were ruined. The
railroads were destroyed. Their few manufacto-
ries were desolated. Their vessels had been swept
from the seas and the rivers. The live-stock was
consumed. Notes, bonds, mortgages, all the
money in circulation, debts, became alike worthless. The community were without clothes and
without food. Every thing had gone into the
rapacious maw of the Confederate Government;
vast estates had crumbled like paper in a fire.
While the shape was not wholly destroyed, the
substance had turned to ashes. Never was there
greater nakedness and desolation in a civilized
community. Added to all this was the loss of
12,000 of the best blood of the State out of a voting population of 60,000—the pride of families and
the hope of the State. They had gone to their
graves, hurried thither by the hot blast of war.
Individual examples of suffering among the oldest and wealthiest families of the State could be
given to any extent—each a tragedy. But this
is not all. The white citizen, dazed with a sudden appreciation of his stripped and bereft condition, when the end came, turned only to behold the extraordinary transformation of his
bondmen. The slave had suddenly acquired his
freedom, and with that the right to vote and
hold office. The enfranchised negroes were a
majority in three-quarters of the counties in the

State. They all at once gathered at the polls, chose themselves to office, and under slight guidance became its rulers and governors. Amazed at the sudden change, stunned by this blow at their pride and power, the whites looked around to see if all was a hideous dream. They found the movement backed by United States bayonets, and then they knew it was a ghastly reality. The civilized and educated white race was under foot, prostrate and powerless, and the black barbarian reigned in its stead. He reigns to-day in the full plenitude of an overwhelming majority, and at every point with unabridged authority. There is not a white minority at the State-House large enough to check legislation in any of its stages, or modify it in any of its phases. The handful of white representatives in the Legislature sit mute spectators of its proceedings, and seem only to exist to witness the tight grip and relentless hold the emancipated slaves keep upon the throats of their old masters. It is the great political novelty of the age, the most conspicuous fact of the slave-holders' rebellion ; a tragedy and a fate more strange than any fiction.

The great and all-important question for South Carolina to canvass and decide is this : What can its substantial, land-holding, honest white citizens do, in the existing emergency, to put an end to the present infamous rule of the

State ? Our answer would be : Let them first fix their eyes upon the great continuous stream of foreign immigration which lands 300,000 people, seeking new homes, annually on our shores—a body self-impelled, and almost wholly self-directed, as yet, but which is capable of being turned, deflected, and changed to a most considerable degree, by efficient measures taken toward that end. No experiment has ever been made to see what strong concerted action might accomplish in this direction. But with such an enormous mass of malleable material to work upon, it is fair to suppose that wise and concerted efforts would be crowned with success. This is the first point to be considered. The second step is to disabuse the South Carolina mind of some erroneous ideas entertained by it in regard to white immigrants. The State having suffered so much from carpetbaggers, it is no wonder the native population look upon strangers with suspicion. But the white immigrant of the future is to recompense her for the carpet-baggers' frauds and spoliations. There is no fear that he will not be on the side of justice and economy, and good government; for it is his interest to be so, as much as it is for the resident white citizen. Only let the white immigrants from all quarters be encouraged to come. Let no man bother himself about the immigrants' opinions. It has been too much the

habit of the old South Carolinian to feel that the
State, in all its franchises, potentialities, and future possibilities, belongs to him and to him
alone, and that it is for him to exercise a sort of
surveillance over the character and opinions of
those who would come and share his opportunities. It used to be said in the old days of slavery, and there is a feeble echo of the sentiment
still left, that South Carolinians will welcome all
who come to the State, provided they come to
promote its industrial prosperity, and leave politics alone. But we all see that this is all out of
place now. South Carolina must grow in the
future, if she is to be redeemed and keep pace
with her sister States, as those States grow, by
the introduction of numbers, and of wealth and
enterprise from without, and they must come
enjoying the same absolute freedom from surveillance and criticism that is enjoyed everywhere else. In these days of mental activity,
the emigrant carries with him, among his other
possessions, a good stock of opinions, and it is
absurd to ask him to lay them down at the fron-
tier of any State which he proposes to make
his future residence. In this respect South Carolina cannot be permitted to enjoy an exemption
granted to no other civilized community on this
continent, and it is preposterous to advance a
suggestion of such a character. If South Caro-

lina is to grow and flourish as other States grow and flourish, she must obey the law of their growth and cheerfully accept its conditions. The fundamental one of all is entire individual independence, and entire individual irresponsibility to others, and to society, as to his conduct and opinions, so long as he is guiltless of all infractions of the law.

It has long been the doctrine of the old slave States that a man should be held personally responsible for the expression of adverse opinions on certain social and political questions. This intolerance of opinion had its roots in the practice of slavery. It survives still in a modified degree, although emancipation has destroyed all apology for it. Any assertion of this spirit in the present changed condition of things is absurd. Every man, in our day, in South Carolina and everywhere else, must be permitted the exercise of his right to the untrammeled expression of his opinion, in decorous terms, on any subject whatever, without rendering himself obnoxious to anybody, or subjecting himself to the rebuke of anybody. This is the one new thing which South Carolina people of high and low degree must be prompt to learn. It is the very first condition of her regeneration and extrication. Nothing short of unreserved submission to this law of all our growing communities will secure the end and objects

5

of her salvation. Immigrants here must be like immigrants everywhere, free, unconstrained, independent. Every invitation to them to come must be conceived in this spirit, and expressed in these terms. They must not be expected to bend to the old ways of an old society, but to proceed by such methods and walk in such paths as shall seem best in their own eyes, however strange and new to all others. There is no alternative for her white population and property-holders but heartily to second these views, or continue to hold their present humiliating position, which means further declension and final ruin to them and their posterity. There is no longer any law of entail for opinions in this country. The war ended that. And it behooves South Carolina to recognize it quickly. She is at the meeting of the waters. She has a great opportunity to retrieve her fortunes. But the chance is equally good to sacrifice them. Those whose duty and business it is to act in this great emergency, may by their inaction, their inertia, let the State slide into ruin, and thus make its future a standing blot on our existing civilization. But, on the other hand, they may avert this result, and give to it a future which shall eclipse all its former glories.

CHAPTER XIV.

Inducements to Immigrants.—Cheap Lands and a Salubrious Climate.—The Profitableness of Cotton Culture.—An Agricultural Paradise.—The History of Previous Migrations.

SOUTH CAROLINA affords great enticements to the agricultural immigrant. Portions of half a dozen of the lower counties toward the seaboard are unhealthy. But two-thirds, or more, of the State is otherwise. This two-thirds embraces a large portion of the cotton-lands, and all the grain-growing and grazing regions. Columbia is very near the geographical centre of the State. Here, the statistics show that the greatest mortality is between November and April, and that the summer heats thus engender no maladies. This rule holds good in all the State north and west of Columbia, and, on the south and east, half-way down to the coast. Several of the towns directly on the seaboard are equally healthy. Charleston claims a smaller mortality than any city of the North, with the single exception of Portland, in Maine.

In addition to this general salubrity, the State

enjoys the inestimable advantage, for an agricultural country, of having no winter. Plowing
may be, and is, carried on in every month of the
year. The average mean temperature of Columbia for the month of February, 1873, at 8 A. M.,
was over 48°, and at 3 P. M. it was a fraction over
60°. I suppose the month of April would not make
as good a showing as this in New England or the
Northwest. But the number of trees and plants
that grow out-of-doors in Columbia, and give such
an exceptional air of verdure to the winter land-
scape, affords proof enough of the mild character
of the climate. Here grow and flourish in the
open air, the *Camellia Japonica*, the *Laurusti-*
nus, the Cape jasmine, the English and Spanish
laurel, the Chinese hawthorn, so called, the hol-
ly, the Chinese and Australian pines, the live-
oaks, the tree-box, the mock-orange, and the
magnificent magnolia, besides various others.
None of the plants or trees I have enumerated
shed their leaves during the winter, and there
need be no finer shade-trees than the mock-
orange and the massive and graceful live-oak.
Columbia is the heart of a great cotton-region.
This crop is cultivated to the exclusion of others
that can be raised with equal facility, though
not with equal profit. There is nothing like
cotton for profit. Land that will not bring ten
bushels of corn to the acre will produce half a

bale of cotton, worth forty to fifty dollars. Nobody can be long in a cotton-growing country
without sharing in the fascinations of its culture,
and, as an agriculturist, abjuring all climates
where it will not grow. There is no labor in
raising it that is not easy and enticing, and it
exhausts the land no more than the thistle-down,
if you but return the seed to the ground. Corn
can be produced as well here as in Pennsylvania.
It has been worth all winter in Columbia over one
dollar a bushel; and hay, which is more difficult to
raise, but which an experienced English gardener
here says he can raise, and has raised, at the rate
of two tons to the acre, simply by heavy top-
dressing, is steadily worth forty-five to fifty dollars a ton in the same market. But it ought to
be said that, except on river-bottoms, grass does
not naturally flourish in a climate where cotton
grows. The summer heats parch and wither it.

There is plenty of old plantation-land in the
market at extremely low prices. Lands that
were held before the war at twenty-five and
thirty dollars an acre, and cheap enough at that,
can now be had at two, three, four, five, and
ten dollars an acre. These lands are all in
working order, and need only good farming to
make them more profitable than they ever were.
The old planters were nearly all ruined or greatly
embarrassed by the war, and those who survive

cannot readily adapt themselves to the changes that emancipation has brought. But labor is plenty, and there seems to be no serious obstacle to a revival of the agriculture of the State on the new basis. The transition is naturally attended by difficulties, but none great enough to conquer ordinary enterprise. With every facility for making such sure and profitable crops as corn and cotton, the temptation to an agriculturist would appear to be very much greater than is offered on the Western prairie-lands. Let any man take a price-current of Western agricultural products at the point where they are raised, and he will be amazed at the comparatively unremunerating figures they show, contrasted with those in South Carolina: Hay six dollars a ton, corn twenty-five cents a bushel, pork four dollars a hundred pounds, and other things in proportion. Let him compare these prices with those of the products of a South Carolina upland plantation, where every thing is as cheerful and healthy as on the best rolling prairies, to say the least; and where there is no winter of sufficient rigor to necessitate either extra clothing or extra fuel, and no weather to impede agricultural occupation at all times of the year. The "middling" or standard grade of South Carolina cotton is at present worth at any railroad-station in the State about eighteen cents a pound. An acre of land will produce from three hundred to five hundred pounds, according to the character of the cultivation, and the crop is as sure and the price as steady, in the long-run, as that of any crop that grows; while no other is so imperishable, or so easily handled, or requires so little room or attention. A crop worth a thousand dollars may be put in a cow-stall. Once gathered and put into bale, it is subjected to no contingencies of weather, or season, or insects. It neither deteriorates nor perishes by waiting, and the holder may thus take his own time to market it. The standing complaint in every cotton-growing country is that farmers will grow nothing else. But this is no wonder. Still, every good farmer will guard himself on this point.

A small farmer on the outskirts of Columbia lately bought eighty acres of land. Last year he put forty acres in cotton. He raised forty bales of five hundred pounds each on these forty acres. He had the advantage of a good supply of stable-manure from the town, and of labor from the same source. The total cost of production was nine cents a pound. He sold his crop on the spot for eighteen or nineteen cents a pound, making a clear profit of nearly fifty dollars a bale. The exceptional advantages which enabled him to do this were an unlimited supply of cotton-hands from the town, who worked for fifty cents a day and " found " themselves, and the control of the manure-product from a livery-stable. But his was not a single example. Another farmer near by, with similar facilities for dressing his land, accomplished the same results. Both were preparing and expecting to do equally well the present season. Now, while every farmer cannot do this, at first, for want of an immediate supply of manure and equal facilities for procuring labor, it may be taken as the standard of profitable farming in the upland country of South Carolina, which every cultivator can approximate under any good system of farming. Considering that the same land will produce corn, grain, and potatoes in abundance, and even grass, it would seem to be difficult to know where an agriculturist could turn to find so good a prospect of reward for his labors. The new discoveries of an unlimited supply of artificial manure in the inexhaustible beds of phosphate about Charleston, come most opportunely at the present time to enable new cultivators to put their lands at once under profitable cultivation. These artificial manures seem to be all that is requisite to enrich the old cotton-lands and restore their productive power.

The Northern people, who, in their eager ignorance, rushed south after the war, thinking to acquire easy and sudden fortunes by raising cotton, were met by bad seasons and a falling

market. Of course they generally failed. No
man can reasonably expect to succeed in any
such *extempore* enterprises. As a rule, the great
agricultural products of the world yield no sudden fortunes even to the experienced cultivator.
How could it have been expected that ignorant
adventurers should reap them in a day? It is
the merit of agriculture, as a pursuit, not that its
profits are great, but that its results are sure and
steady, and increase just in proportion to the skill
and industry of the cultivator. Its attractions
are its pleasing conditions. And if there be an
elysium for an agriculturist, it is a fruitful soil, a
salubrious climate, and a delicious atmosphere
in which frosts and snows are almost unknown.
These are the advantages South Carolina proffers.

The State is thrown open anew to immigrants
by the accidental conditions of society and industry caused by the war. And the advantages
offered were never greater than now. There
have been two principal migrations into the State
in times past. One after the battle of Culloden,
and one after the Irish rebellion of 1798. They
were composed mainly of Scotch and Scotch-Irish.
Both were successful, and both have made their
mark on the State; some of its most eminent
names having been descended from them. There
is no reason why there should not be another,
still more successful than any preceding one.

Intelligent combined action of the present race of depressed and robbed land-owners could surely effect it. They have the power to restore the just equilibrium of the races, and remove the offensive political anomaly that now exists. This ability, and the enticements to agricultural immigration that have been thus briefly suggested, afford a solid expectation that South Carolina will retrieve the dominion of intelligence and probity in her political life, and enter upon a career of material prosperity greater than any she has ever yet experienced.

CHAPTER XV.

Some Detached Observations.

MANY of the old families remain in Columbia, but they are no longer rich, and keep themselves secluded from the general current of affairs. Their places, which used to be tidy and bright, are growing shabby and dilapidated, and the occupants live on their departed glories and what they have been able to save from the wreck of their estates.

They are like the old St. Germain aristocracy during the latter Empire, who used to say of Louis Napoleon and the promiscuous crowd who occupied the Tuileries in his reign, "We know none of these people."

The old Wade Hampton mansion, built by the head of the family of Revolutionary memory, which is the best establishment in Columbia, has just passed out of the hands of the third generaration of the family that so long occupied it. It has been sold to the new plebeian Governor, Moses, an Israelite, who, having a thrifty eye to the main chance, left the old aristocracy and joined the new democracy, in which he now holds the chief place. It is one of those somersaults that tend largely to exalt our estimate of the dignity of human nature. Colonel Preston, the late owner and occupier of the place, espoused a scion of the house, and now returns to his native Virginia, whence the family, which has achieved eminence in South Carolina, originally emigrated.

It is estimated that 1,100 buildings were burned in Columbia at the period of Sherman's march, many of them the best dwellings in the city. The main business street, in which nearly all the buildings were destroyed, has been to a considerable extent rebuilt, but it is not so with the remainder of the town, where many vacant squares exist. Some of the money stolen from the Treasury is being employed in erecting stately edifices on the main street.

Among the less hopeful of the future of South Carolina are those who suggest a division of the State, giving one portion to Georgia and another to North Carolina, in order to get rid of the predominance of the colored element. But this does not seem to be a feasible scheme. It is hard to see how a State is to be obliterated without the consent of its people, and the consent of the black man is not likely to be obtained to any such swamping process as this. It is not likely his vote could be purchased for this object, though all the Pattersons and Camerons of the country were here to consummate the trade.

Sambo dotes on legislative committees. The struggle to get on those that pay best is amusing. The House, in their eagerness and greed, have, it is said, increased the Railroad Committee to some eighteen members. Then they have strolling committees. One was sent to New York to report on the state of the debt, and, it is alleged, cost the State $200,000. He is regarded as a happy man who gets on one of these committees. But success begets jealousy. Some of the new members are beginning to call a halt on the old ones. The latter are thought to have had too much already. The Senate was lately the scene of some of these collisions, and the old crowd were snubbed by the new. The feeling all through the Legislature is that the State has been outrageously robbed, but they are utterly in the dark as to how much, or precisely in every case by whom. There is a constant complaint that nobody can find out what the State owes, and the majority is bribed to keep the fact a secret. There is a lively sense of the presence of those who a few years ago were penniless, and now own and live in expensive mansions, and who built and own the iron bridge that spans the broad river that flows past the town, and are erecting opera-houses and warehouses on the main streets; but there are numerous others not so well known. In fact, the suspicion is that pretty much everybody is implicated in a greater or less degree.

A challenge was flung out lately on the white immigration question by a lusty black man who likes to display his aggressive temper. He proposed to his white brethren to bring on their immigrants. He did not fear them. They would find the blacks ready. It was very plain, however, that the white members were not ready for any agitation of the topic in this strain. On this, as on all subjects bearing on the present and future relationships of the races, the whites are wholly reserved and reticent, and apparently fearful.

There are some individuals among the colored members who are so nearly white that no one would suspect colored blood in their veins. They are showy talkers of great animation of manner, with the same spread-eagle style that marks so much of the oratory of wholly white men. They are not amenable to the criticism bestowed on the average African-Americans of the body, for they talk intelligibly and intelligently.

In the Legislature there is a tendency to retrenchment and reform in such points as the expenditures in the departments, and on appropriations generally; the members had to promise this in the late canvass. But the economies are rather nominal than real, as the gross appropriations this year exceed those of the previous year.

It has been made a question whether the property-holders of the State would not save money by giving every sable representative a house and lands, that he might personally taste the sweets of taxation. This would seem to be the only way of bringing it home to him. If it were not that the term of service were so short, the proposition would be worth considering.

It is not harsh to criticise members of this black Parliament in the way we do, for we only say of them what they say of themselves. They are in the habit of charging one another with ignorance and venality and corruption without stint, and it is not deemed any offense. The thieves were obliged, as we have said, to make a sort of compact with their supporters at the last election that they would stop robbing the State.

But like the drunkard who promised to quit drinking, and still drank to intoxication by spells, and defended himself by saying he "always excepted his sprees," so these legislative robbers claim the right to extort pay from everybody who is to profit by their legislation, taking the ground that it is no violation of their pledges, when a senatorial election comes round, to sell their votes to the highest bidder. This is not corruption in their sense of the term. It is only to turn an honest penny.

In regard to all such shameless acts as this, and the refusing of charters to responsible persons to make needed improvements in the State because the members are not bribed, the respectable white men of the Legislature say they should blush with shame if they felt that the real character of the State was represented in the body. But as it is, they can only plead that scoundrelism is dominant, and that all legislation is in the hands of unscrupulous knaves who belong in the penitentiary. The facts fill every decent citizen with mortification, but, outside the gang who hold control, every one claims exemption from all responsibility for the degradation into which the State has fallen.

The only drawback to the country, the only hinderance to an immediate accession of population from the best agricultural classes abroad, is this scoundrel government, which has so long rioted, and is yet rioting, in its robberies. There seems to be no way of even checking their intolerable practices but to flash the flambeaux of an outside execration in their faces. They defy the indignation of the people they have ruined, but they are not proof against the indignation of the country at large. It becomes a public duty

"To lash the rascals naked through the land,"

and aid this prostrate State to recover possession

of itself, retrieve its standing before the world, and drag to condign punishment the culprits who have so long rioted in its spoils, and who so persistently prey upon its remains.

CHAPTER XVI.

Who burned Columbia?—Ruin of the Old Families.—Entire Loss of Property by Rich and Poor.—Individual Cases of Suffering and Destitution.

THERE has been a good deal of controversy as to who burned Columbia. But it is quite superfluous. The facts are clear. Wade Hampton burned the bridge that spanned the river at this point, and the railroad depots, and he ordered all the cotton in town to be burned. This he admits. But he says he countermanded the orders about the cotton, and they were not executed. We may disbelieve this, without impugning his veracity. For our commanders say the cotton and the town were on fire when they entered it. General Hampton idly shelled Sherman's troops lying in bivouac, by night, across the river. These measures were the offspring of mere spite. They had no military significance. When Sherman's troops entered the city they were exasperated, and took their revenge by setting additional fires. Sherman gave no orders to burn the town; and Wade Hampton, who commanded the handful of Confederate troops, says he gave none. But Sherman's men were never mild in South Carolina. They went there to make war, and they made it, sometimes not according to strict rule. But the Confederate commanders have no cause to complain. They did the same. They burned every thing right and left whenever they evacuated a place. Such, for example, was the case in Charleston. On leaving, they not only burned property, but they burned the valuable bridges across the Ashley River, from mere wantonness, harming nobody but their own people. The destruction served no warlike purpose, and was scarcely an inconvenience to the Federal troops. It was just the same in numerous other instances. The example was dangerously contagious, and would naturally be followed, even in the absence of other provocations. The war burned Columbia.

The Southern woman, as she often appeared in the war, was not an object of great admiration to the national troops. But there were numerous specimens of good sense and judgment among them that but slowly reveal themselves. One was a widow of forty. Her husband was a substantial citizen worth half a million. He died in the early part of the war. His brother was made executor of the will. The wife begged him to keep out of Confederate securities. She had no faith in them. She desired the estate to be placed beyond the reach of the calamity which she felt was coming. He pooh-poohed her suggestions, and paid no heed to her admonitions. Her fortune went with the common tide, and her half million was consumed. She saved something on her own account, and always converted her Confederate money into gold. When Sherman reached Savannah she looked on the map, and with the same sagacious judgment that she exhibited in the beginning, she determined that his next move would be on Columbia, although the town was then filled with fugitives from Charleston, seeking shelter and a safe retreat. She emptied her house of its furniture, bought a full stock of provisions and groceries with her Confederate money, loaded the railroad cars with her possessions, and left for the mountains. Her final act was to exchange her last remaining bundle of Confederate notes for gold at the rate of sixty dollars in paper for one dollar in specie, astonishing her broker by the expression of her opinion that, in the next month, it would take one hundred dollars of paper to buy one dollar in gold, and that a month later a bushel-basket full of it wouldn't buy one dollar. Sherman came, and her dwelling disappeared in the flames, but the proprietress was elsewhere. This is the story, in brief, of one of the most fortunate of the rich

families of South Carolina. A small remainder
of a great estate was here snatched from the general conflagration by the sagacity and courage of
a native Southern woman. But usually the great
catastrophe was not foreseen. Every thing went
into Confederate securities; every thing to eat
and every thing to wear was consumed, and when
the war suddenly ended there was nothing left
but absolute poverty and nakedness. Famine
followed, and suffering beyond computation, the
story of which has never been told. Rich planters' families subsisted on corn-bread when they
could get it, but often they could not, and then
they resorted to a coarse cattle-fodder known as
" cow-peas." It is reported of the poet Timrod,
who contributed his fiery lyrics in aid of the rebellion—all that he had to give—that he and his
were saved from actual starvation, when they
were at their last gasp, just previous to his death.
Others fared not so well.

There were numerous large slave-holders and
property-owners in and about Columbia who went
down in the general ruin. Some were immensely
wealthy; there were several families owning 500
and 1,000 slaves apiece. Many were proprietors
of plantations on the banks of the Mississippi.
These plantations were more or less mortgaged.
When slavery went, the mortgages consumed the
rest; and men enjoying an income of $100,000 a

year on the opening of the war were stripped of
their last cent at its close.   An elderly gentleman
of nearly eighty years, formerly a rich man, and
president of a bank of about $1,000,000 capital,
was able by great exertion to save his dwelling
from the conflagration in Columbia.   It was all
he preserved from the wreck of his fortunes.   Hap-
pily he was a lover of flowers, and had a large
greenhouse in his gardens.   In his stripped condition, he resorted to it for support; and to-day
he lives by personally growing flowers for sale,
which he does with a cheerful assiduity that gilds
his misfortunes, and lends even a pleasing glow
to the evening of his life.   Old Wade Hampton,
of Revolutionary memory, who won his spurs at
the battle of Eutaw Springs, and was an aid-de-
camp of General Washington, was a resident of
Columbia, and owned vast estates.   He and his
family were the grandees of their county for all
these subsequent generations.   They numbered
their slaves by the thousand when the war began,
and had large plantations in other States.   The
family is now broken and scattered.   The great
old family mansion and extensive grounds filled
with rare exotics, the abode of luxurious hospi-
tality for seventy years, has, since the war, been
haunted by ghosts, and now, dilapidated and falling into decay, passes into the hands of strangers.
In the vicinity lived a gentleman whose income,

when the war broke out, was rated at $150,000 a year. He was not only a victim to the general ruin, but peculiar circumstances added to his misfortunes. Not a vestige of his whole vast property of millions remains to-day. Not far distant were the estates of a large proprietor and a well-known family, rich and distinguished for generations. The slaves are gone. The family is gone. A single scion of the house remains, and he peddles tea by the pound and molasses by the quart, on a corner of the old homestead, to the former slaves of the family, and thereby earns his livelihood.

These are sample cases merely, that can be easily multiplied, as we may readily conceive, when we remember that the average size of the plantations in South Carolina, at the census of 1860, was no less than 1,600 acres.

But the poor people were stripped as well as the rich. Though they had but little, yet that little was their all. And to lose it was to lose all. And to this was to be added a grievous disappointment. They were selling their butter for fifty dollars a pound, and their chickens for sixty dollars a pair, in Confederate notes, and they were hoarding their imaginary money, feeling they were sure to come out rich in the end. Great was their dismay and their astonishment when they found they had leaned on a broken reed, and their visions of sudden wealth had vanished in an instant.

CHAPTER XVII.

The Frauds of the State Government.

THERE would seem to be no species of public fraud unknown to, and unpractised by, the men who have been in possession of the government of South Carolina since the close of the war.

A simple narrative of events, about which there is no dispute, is perhaps the briefest, as it is the most effectual, way of enabling the reader to form an unbiassed judgment upon the transactions that have occurred.

In what we have now to say, we draw largely from that authentic record, known as the "Report of the Joint Select Committee to inquire into the Condition of Affairs in the late Insurrectionary States, made to the two Houses of Congress, February 10, 1872."

From the mass of testimony presented in that report, and from the views of the majority and minority expressed therein, we extract what bears upon the case, aiming to eliminate every thing of a merely partisan character.

The principal frauds practised in South Carolina come under several heads, which we will treat separately. They are—

1. Those which relate to the increase of the State debt.

2. The frauds practised in the purchase of lands for the freedmen.

3. The railroad frauds.

4. The election frauds.

5. The frauds practised in the redemption of the notes of the Bank of South Carolina.

6. The census fraud.

7. The fraud in furnishing the legislative chambers.

8. General and legislative corruption.

6

CHAPTER XVIII.

On the Frauds which relate to the Increase of the State Debt.

WE have elsewhere stated that, in round numbers, the State debt of South Carolina has been increased from $5,000,000 to $15,000,000 since the war closed.

It turns out in this, as in almost every other point, that the fuller the investigation the worse the disclosures. The debt is a great deal more than $15,000,000, with nothing to show for it.

There is a general agreement over the fact, as will be seen by the statements which follow, that the whole State debt, as late as 1867, was, in round numbers, $5,400,000. To which should be added computed over-due interest and exchange to the amount of $384,000. But in this statement we make no account of a contingent liability of the State, at that time and now, of nearly $3,000,000 as indorser of the bonds of the South Carolina Railroad, and the Savannah & Charleston Railroad, corporations understood to be perfectly solvent. These we therefore dismiss from our estimates and calculations.

Neither do we reckon in this estimate the old liability of the State for certain bills of circulation of the Bank of the State of South Carolina, to the amount of over $1,250,000, which will appear elsewhere, and which since the war have been disposed of by a specific issue of State bonds for $1,590,000; the difference between these two sums having been apparently stolen by the manipulators of the transaction.

Governor Scott was inaugurated in July, 1868. The actual State debt, excluding the items mentioned, was, just previous to that time, as we have seen, a little less than $5,800,000.

But it owed some current liabilities for interest and expenses, the legacy of the anomalous period preceding Scott's advent. Just what these amounted to, does not appear. All we know is, that the first Legislature under Scott's administration, in August, 1868, passed two acts appropriating $1,600,000 to pay interest money, and relieve the wants of the Treasury, and in the following February (1869) appropriated $1,000,000 for the same purpose.

These sums were designed to tide over the crisis. But, although these are said to be the only authorized bonds of the State issued for general purposes, a very large amount of bonds was ordered of and printed by the American Bank Note Company of New York, amounting in all to $22,500,000, for which the State authorities are answerable.

If to this $22,500,000 we add previously-existing bonds, we have an apparent aggregate of $27,900,000, as the bonded debt of the State.

Whether these bonds are all on the market is unknown. Attempts have been made from time to time in the Legislature to get at the facts, but they have always been frustrated. At the late session, ending in March, 1873, an effort was made to induce the Legislature to pass a bill, calling upon all holders of State bonds to bring them forward for registration, in order that the actual sum issued might be known and established. But so deep was the demoralization of that body, that it was suborned into giving its refusal to the passage of this salutary measure, by those who have profited by the fraudulent issue of the bonds, and who are not ready for the consequences that would necessarily ensue from such an exposition.

In addition to this issue of twenty-seven million nine hundred thousand dollars ($27,900,000), the Legislature of 1868–'69 passed an act guaranteeing the bonds of the Blue Ridge Railroad to the amount of $4,000,000, and also an act guaranteeing the bonds of the Greenville & Columbia Railroad to the amount of about $2,000,000.

The names of the parties engaged, and the

character of these two transactions, will be found in a following chapter.

Since the period of these acts and the subsequent investigation of the facts in the reports herein quoted, the State government has been engaged in business of a similar character, which adds constantly to the magnitude of the debt. It is understood that the late Speaker (now Governor) did, while in his former office, issue some $400,000 of pay certificates, for which the Treasury is now liable. There has also been authorized a scrip issue of the Blue Ridge Railroad, of $1,800,000, thrown into circulation by being made receivable for taxes, thus consuming the available funds of the State, and swelling its indebtedness in a form which exacts increased taxation. As the operation was purely speculative, and designed only as a raid on the Treasury, without any design of resuscitating a defunct concern, it is quite in character that a report should now be rife, not only that the $1,800,000 of scrip has been issued, but that there have been three times that sum issued, in three independent sets of securities. But, adding only the $6,000,000 of indebtedness of the two railroads before mentioned, and we have an estimated aggregate State debt of thirty-three million nine hundred thousand dollars ($33,900,000).

There is an allegation that some of the bonds

that go to create this indebtedness have never
been issued, but are lying in the Treasury and in
the hands of the Bank Note Company. And in
the various estimates of the debt by the State Legislative committee of investigation, and by the
congressional committee, detailed in the following
pages, there has been sometimes more and sometimes less credence given to those allegations.

The only safe way, in our opinion, to estimate
the bonded debt, is to take the whole amount of
the bonds executed by the Bank Note Company
on the orders of the Scott government, and add
it to the previous outstanding bonds. These two
sums make $27,900,000. The fact that the par-
ties implicated in the known large fraudulent issues, bribed the Legislature to refuse an investigation into the actual facts, shows that the "confessed
debt" of $16,371,000, shown in the legislative
committee's report, is a false exhibit. If it were
not, why should they decline the proposition to
have it verified? But there is another way of
proving the overwhelming indebtedness of the
State, that admits of no question.

Since the examination referred to in the following pages was made, another fiscal year has
elapsed, and we have the report of the Treasurer
and Controller for the year ending November,
1872.

This report shows, in its general debtor and

creditor statement, that the State owes, on bonded and current indebtedness, which has found its way on to the books of the Treasury, the sum of $26,621,000. Of this it owes the Bank of the State of South Carolina $1,839,000. But the statement also shows that the State has sundry credits with that institution; of money, of sinking-fund securities, of bank-stock, etc. In estimating the State's affairs for this occasion, we strike out all its accounts with the bank, both debt and credit. We take it for granted it has no actual assets there, for the reason that it has no available or real assets anywhere, as they have all been exhausted long ago.

Striking out, then, this item of indebtedness to the bank, which we will allow to be offset by its credits, though it is quite possible this makes too favorable a showing for the State, we find the following result, as the upshot of the Controller's report :

Whole State indebtedness	$26,621,917 00
Deduct due to bank	1,839,011 00
Total	$24,782,906 00

Leaving an outstanding debt of twenty-four million seven hundred and eighty-three thousand dollars ($24,783,000) in round numbers.

Now, on an examination of the resources of the State in the Treasury, as presented by the oppo-

site side of the ledger in this report, we find that
the aggregate of available funds, consisting of
debts of collectors, county treasurers, and other
officers, and uncollected taxes, and all other
available resources; counting every thing which
appears in the shape of debt, to be good,
this aggregate, we say, amounts to just about
$1,000,000. So that, according to the showing
of the books of the Treasury, the State owes
a round sum of twenty - four million dollars
($24,000,000).

What the amount of unreckoned and unac-
knowledged obligations of the State is, that have
not yet found their way on to the books of the
Treasury, we have no means of knowing. Neither
do we know how many of the State bonds of the
$22,500,000 printed by the New York Bank Note
Company, are yet to be added to the quantity on
record as having been already issued. The mys-
terious action of the parties implicated in their
emission, and their aversion to having the issues
verified, excite well-founded suspicion that this
record of the indebtedness of the State will have
to be much increased when all the facts are
known.

It should be added that the indebtedness calculated above includes a war debt of about $2,-
500,000, which will ultimately have to be stricken
out of the accounts. But the accruing interest on

the debt, and the charging up of as yet unrecognized obligations, will not be long in supplying its place.

It should also be said that the debt shown on the Controller's books takes no account of the obligations of the State in its indorsement of the $6,000,000 of bonds of the Blue Ridge and Columbia & Greenville Railroads, which is so much more to be added to the aggregate of $24,000,000, and for which there is no security.

The figures of the Controller's report show an enormous floating debt, and if it should turn out that the whole of the State bonds printed have really gone into circulation through a surreptitious issue, the amount of the State debt will be several millions beyond the highest sum we have named.

With this preliminary exposition, we give way to the introduction of the testimony, the comments, and the conclusions of the State legislative committee, and of the joint committee of Congress, who investigated the subject in 1872.

The following is the statement of the committee of investigation of the South Carolina Legislature, appointed by the Republicans:

The actual debt, then, if the "severe personal scrutiny" of the Governor "is correct," is as follows, viz.:

Debt of the State, July, 1868, less $9,000 old bonds
    redeemed..................................... $5,398,306 27

Bonds issued in 1869, for funding bills of Bank of
    the State of South Carolina.................   1,259,000 00

Bonds represented to have been delivered H. H.
    Kimpton, financial agent, New York........   9,514,000 00

To which must be added the bonds for which the
    college land scrip sold, now in the hands of
    the financial agent, which cannot be less than   200,000 00

And we have a total confessed debt of........... $16,371,306 27

To this can be safely added the sterling loan
    bonds "deposited for safe-keeping," subject
    to order, $3,500,000, of which have been
    signed and made ready for issue, and the
    arrangements perfected for the negotiation
    of the entire loan, unless the law authorizing
    the said bonds is immediately repealed, and
    the bonds canceled before they can be nego-
    tiated, viz..................................   6,000,000 00

Which would give an aggregated old and new
    bonded debt of..................—........   22,371,306 27

To which add the contingent debt, viz..........   6,787,608 20

And the entire indebtedness of the State is...... $29,158,914 47

Of this amount it is said there are in the hands of
    the financial agent, as collateral security for
    loans, $3,773,000 of new bonds, and a deduc-
    tion of that amount is claimed from the whole
    amount of new bonds in use ; but, as collat-
    erals, they are virtually a part of the debt,
    until the loans for which they are held are re-
    deemed or paid. From which deduct author-
    ized bonds, including sterling loan, viz......   22,844,914 47

And the fraudulent issue is $6,314,000 00

The committee assure the General Assembly they are
confident no one could have labored more assiduously or
thoroughly than they have done in the work of investi-

gation of the various financial departments of the State, as well as other avenues of discovery. They do not feel, however, that they can safely say they have given the whole extent of extravagance or criminal indulgence with which the management of the funds and credit of the State has been characterized. There is an unknown "floating debt;" the financial agent is still unpaid; he is to present his "honest claims" proportioned to his "faithful service." And, as millions have been tossed about in the multiplied transactions of this "experienced and competent" financier, small considerations will be no "compensation" to him; *liberal satisfaction* must be awarded; and if the lithograph-electrotype printing-press has not piled up, in bonds or stocks, sufficient already to cancel his, with other illegitimate demands, and his greedy hold upon the State is not loosened, then millions more must be added to the gigantic dimensions of "what we are responsible for," so far as printed illegalities can make us. The committee, in view of the atrocity of these disclosures—the work of the present administration, or rather a ring composed of leading officers of the government of the State, unhesitatingly say that the Republican party, which has elevated them to power, must show its condemnation of such treachery and knavery by an immediate and united effort—by legislative enactments, as well as by every other deliberate measure—to bring to justice those who have prostituted the authority with which they have been clothed, and so flagrantly and criminally imperiled the trusts to them confided.

The millions that have been put in their hands could not have been authorized or manipulated for honest purposes, but for plunder and dishonest gain. It is in vain that the public is appealed to with statements that this frightful discovery "is a groundless misrepresentation and gross frabrication." The American Bank Note Company

gives us the figures; they speak for themselves, and tell us
that there have been printed the following bonds and stocks:

Bonds and coupons to pay interest on public debt....	$2,000,000
Bonds and coupons to redeem bills receivable........	500,000
Bonds and coupons to redeem bills of Bank of State of South Carolina...............................	1,590,000
Bonds and coupons for the relief of the Treasury.....	1,000,000
Bonds and coupons for conversion of State securities.	8,200,000
Bonds and coupons for the land commission..........	700,000
Bonds and coupons for sterling funded debt.........	6,000,000
Registered certificates of stock......................	2,550,000
Total..............................	$22,540,000

Of this amount there has been sent by the American
Bank Note Company to the Governor, $2,350,000; to the
Treasurer, $17,490,000; to the Controller-General, $200,-
000, and there remains in the hands of the Bank Note
Company, subject to order, $2,500,000. It has been said
by the authors of this enormous fraud, as if to blind the
true intent of the extravagant issue, that, "although such
an amount of bonds had been printed, all had not been
issued nor signed, nor had they been printed with the
intention of increasing the State debt, but are in possession of the State authorities."

Such a declaration, like a desperate confession, is the
strongest evidence of guilt; it is too transparent to convince even the most credulous. "What was the object of
printing these bonds," has been asked, "if it was not the
intention to use them?" If there is no informality in
the transaction, why let the credit of the State be hazard-
ed by withholding the actual amount of these bonds now
upon the market? Why need such a sum be in the hands
of the State authorities? What object have they in pos-
sessing more than the laws authorizing the respective loans
have called for? Is there any statute authorizing an

indefinite printing of bonds "to be in the possession of the State authorities" to be used at will? Can the acts of the Legislature to pay the indebtedness of the State, or for the conversion of its securities, be construed into such a wholesale prerogative? Is there a necessity to provide more bonds than there are needs for them? Plainly, must we declare we cannot believe other than the fearful truth that stares us in the face, that the bonds and stocks printed by the American Bank Note Company represent the liabilities of the State, for which the faith and credit of the State, however unlawfully presented, has been pledged for the payment; that, instead of the debt of the State of South Carolina being, as the Controller-General in his report for the fiscal year ending October 31, 1871, says, $7,665,708.98; or as Mr. Trenholm, of the Tax-payers' Convention, gives it, viz., $9,869.108; or as the governor, in his statement to the congressional committee, makes it, viz., $9,528,964.10; or as the present committee, from the investigation of erroneous accounts, have, in the previous pages, shown, viz., $9,865,908.98; it is, allowing all the deductions to be made that, in October last, while in New York, were claimed should be, not less than $14,040,000, without the addition of the present contingent liabilities of the State, viz., $6,787,608.20, which would represent a debt of $20,787,608.20.

In order that those who are implicated may be fairly dealt with, the committee will give the benefit, in their report, of their claims for deductions.

It is said the sterling loan bonds should be deducted, as they have been returned by the treasurer to the American Bank Note Company, viz.................................... $3,500,000

Also, bonds for the conversion of State securities printed by mistake of the Bank Note Company, with green backs instead of blue, (the uniform color,) to the amount of......................... 500,000

Brought forward	$4,000,000
Also, the first issue of the bonds for the payment of the interest on the public debt, which, having those words printed on their face, would, the financial agent thought, if issued, injure the credit of the State; therefore, by his recommendation, an equal amount, with the words, "Authorized by act approved August 26, 1868," upon their face, were printed; this deduction claimed is................	1,000,000
Also, the conversion bonds delivered the Treasurer October 4 and 11, 1871, which the Governor refused to sign, viz.......................................	1,000,000
Also, the balance of sterling loan bonds waiting signature and orders for delivery, already printed and in the hands of the American Bank Note Company, viz...	2,500,000
Total of deduction claimed....................	$8,500,000

which, from the $22,540,000 already given, reduce the bonds and stocks for which the authors say the State is accountable, and the Governor, in his unlucid moments, while in New York, intimated might be correct, viz., $14,040,000.

They concluded their report thus, beginning on page 266 and ending on 269:

Since the foregoing was prepared for the press, the State Treasurer, as well as "Citizens' Investigating Committee," made their statements, and the Governor, in his last message to the General Assembly, November 28, 1871, reiterates them, in order to relieve the public mind "and correct the gross exaggerations that are being diligently circulated in reference to our finances and the entire administration of the State." Allowing all they have claimed in their printed report, viz., that there have been destroyed, canceled, deposited for safe keeping, and on hand in the State Treasury, bonds to the amount of $13,026,000, then the entire bonded debt, actual and contingent, is $21,708,914.47, from which deduct contingent

railroad bonds, viz., $6,787,608.20, and the real bonded
debt, is $14,921,306.37; from which also deduct the old
bonded debt, or the debt as it existed when the present
financial managers came into power, viz, $5,407,306.27, and
they reveal the extravagant and unwarranted issue of bonds
and stocks (since their mismanagement of the finances)
of no less than $9,514,000, which is just the amount rep-
resented to have been delivered to the financial agent in
New York. An issue of nearly $2,000,000 more than
the whole bonded debt, old and new, as exhibited in the
Controller-General's statement, October 31, 1871, and
within $355,108 of the entire debt, as stated by Mr.
George Trenholm to the Tax-payers' Convention, and only
$14,964.10 less than Governor Scott declared to the con-
gressional investigating committee in September last, was
the total issue of bonds and stock from June, 1868, to
September 20, 1871, after deducting the bonds and stock
issued for military defense. It will be remembered that
the various acts authorizing loans since the inauguration of
the present government admit of an issue of $3,000,000;
and that the act for the conversion of the State securities
was not supposed to be an authority to increase the debt
already legalized, but a provision of law to convert all
outstanding issues into one uniform class of bonds, the old
bonds to be canceled when the conversion bonds were
issued. Such a course, however, has not been pursued.
The managers were seemingly determined not to keep the
liabilities of the State at their legal standard, but by the
new process of conversion to create a larger amount of
bonds as collaterals, while they mendaciously declared that
the debt was not enlarged. The bonds converted were
not canceled, but still used and hypothecated, and by the
financial agent, whose instructions or directions could
come from no other source than the financial board. If

we, then, from the $9,514,000 of bonds placed in the financial agent's hands, deduct the legally authorized bonds, viz., $3,200,000, we find an illegal over-issue of $6,314,000.

Here, then, we have the indisputable evidence that all the financial officers of the State, as well as the Governor himself, in their State and official papers, have hitherto disguised the true condition of the debt, as well as the issue of bonds, and we have the Executive confession that he too was deceived, and that all his debt statements, up to September last, " were made according to the best of his knowledge at those dates."

But the fact which now presents itself shows that his Excellency's knowledge in September last was sadly deficient, or the excess in bonds and stocks over his statement at that date, now apparent, has been created since. However, as no bonds or stocks could be authorized or issued without his knowledge, the conclusion must be, that, while " charging upon others any just share of their responsibilities for the evil consequences of their acts," he has somewhat "hesitated fully to admit his own." Nor can his final " severe personal scrutiny" convince us that the Treasurer's last exhibit of the actual debt of the State is full and correct.

It is admitted now, which never would have been done had not the joint special financial investigating committee discovered the fact, about the last of October, that the Governor and Treasurer of the State authorized the American Bank Note Company to print various bonds and stocks, amounting to $22,540,000, all of which, at the time of the discovery, had been delivered to the Governor, Treasurer, and Controller-General, except $2,500,000 of the sterling loan bonds, which were waiting the orders of the proper officials.

In conclusion, if, through what has been revealed herein, the innocent, by their intimate or official relationship which they have held with the perpetrators of these wholesale frauds, suffer an equal condemnation with the guilty, let the arraignment of the robbers be speedy, and their punishment as sure. The terrible wrongs committed demand that judgment shall be meted out at once. Position nor place should delay the work of strict accountability. Let the axe fall upon the heads of corrupt officials, however high their prerogatives. The credit of the State, its honor, its future respect, every thing that makes the people of a Commonwealth worthy esteem or commendation —her trusts betrayed, her pledges violated, the frauds committed in her name, by reckless, shameless traducers and plunderers—all cry out for justice. Let no moment be lost in the exercise of duty. The dominant party must recognize the responsibility now resting upon its shoulders, and deal with bad men, though they may be their acknowledged leaders, as exact justice demands, or witness the sceptre of their power pass from their hands amid the execrations of an outraged and indignant people.

TAX-PAYERS' REPORT.

On the 12th of May, 1871, the tax-payers convention, which met at Columbia, reported the following :

THE PUBLIC DEBT OF THE STATE.

The following is a statement of the bonds and stock of the State on which its name appears, outstanding, as near as could be ascertained during the short session of the convention :

Amount of bonds and stock outstanding on the 1st of October, 1867, as exhibited by the report of the Controller-General for November, 1867, exclusive of bonds issued for military defense...................... $5,407,215 23

To this must be added the difference between the true amount due on the fire-loan sterling bonds past due, unpaid and payable in London, to wit, $788,222.27, and that stated in the Controller-General's report, to wit, $484,444.51.................. 383,777 76
                                                          ——————— $5,790,992 99

Amount due on bonds issued under acts of 1860 and 1861 for military defense, as by comptroller's report for October, 1867........................... 2,854,679 78
                                                          ———————

Total as principal of October, 1867........... $8,645,672 77

Bonds issued by present administration as follows:

Under act approved August 26, 1868, for redemption of bills receivable. $500,000 00

Under act approved August 26, 1868, for payment of interest on public debt 1,100,000 00

Under act approved September 15, 1868, for funding bills of the Bank of the State of South Carolina..... 1,258,550 00

Under act approved February 17, 1869, for relief of the Treasury......... 1,000,000 00

Under act approved March 27, 1869, for Land Commission............. 200,000 00

Under act approved March 1, 1870, for Land Commission 500,000 00
                                                          ——————— $4,558,550 00

Total outstanding obligations of the State as principal $13,204,222 77

Statement of Contingent Liabilities of the State of South Carolina arising from the indorsement of railroad bonds:

South Carolina Railroad bonds, payable in 1868, secured by first mortgage	$2,093,312 40
Charleston & Savannah Railroad bonds, payable in 1877, secured by first mortgage	505,000 00
Savannah & Charleston Railroad bonds, under act of 1869, payable in 1869, secured by first mortgage..	245,750 00
Laurens Railroad bonds, payable in 1879, secured by first mortgage....	75,000 00
Spartanburg & Union Railroad bonds, payable in 1878-'79, secured by first mortgage	350,000 00
Greenville & Columbia Railroad bonds and certificates of indebtedness, payable in 1881, 1882, 1883, and 1888, under acts of 1861, 1866, and 1869, secured by first mortgage	1,426,545 80
Blue Ridge Railroad bonds, under act of 1868	4,000,000 00

$8,695,608 20

Indebtedness of the State as principal and guarantor, inclusive of bonds issued for military defense $22,899,830 97

Less amount due as of October, 1867, on bonds issued for military defense...................... 2,854,679 78

Indebtedness of the State as principal and guarantor, exclusive of war-debt...................... $20,045,151 19

Judge Poland, of the congressional committee, speaks of the debt in the following paragraphs of his report :

The controversy existing in this State as to the amount

of its debt illustrates the spirit of partisan opposition to the State government by those who complain of the increase of debt, and at the same time the utterly indefensible conduct of the officers of the State, which renders such a question doubtful or even difficult of a clear, honest, and conclusive solution.

The obstacles with which the State government has to deal in the bitterness of hostility evinced to its every act, is manifest when the testimony of those who complain of the increase of State debt is examined. Take, for instance, that of Judge Carpenter: in the increase of State debt attributed to Governor Scott's administration, he includes $500,000 of bonds issued to meet the debt incurred during the previous administration of Provisional Governor Orr; $1,000,000 of bonds issued to pay the interest of the former debt of the State which accumulated during the war and remained unpaid; and $1,259,000 of bonds issued to redeem the notes of the State Bank, for which the faith of the State was pledged. These were all debts existing before Governor Scott's administration began, but they are classed with the burdens which the State is bearing under his rule. It is to be remarked also that a portion of the State Bank bills were issued during the war, and ought to be rejected as issued for war purposes, but, the amount being uncertain, they were included in those to be redeemed. This much of the debt was clearly forbidden to be paid by the terms of the fourteenth amendment; but that ground of objection was not urged by any of the complainants. But, on the other hand, the statements made by the Governor, the Controller, by the State Treasurer, and financial agent of the State, vary so much from the statements derived from other sources claiming to have knowledge of the actual amount of the debt, of the over-issue of bonds, and of the hypothecation of others, that the real amount of debt seems to be an unsettled problem, involving Governor, Treasurer, and State agent in charges of dishonest and unlawful conduct, and presenting a state of such uncertainty, upon a question which the records of the State ought to settle at once upon examination, that the existence of the controversy is in itself disgraceful to all these officers, and cannot but be disastrous to the credit and interests of the Commonwealth.

We append the explanation of Governor Scott in regard to the large increase of the State indebtedness, and also the comments of the congressional committee thereon, in a report from the Hon. J. E. Stevenson. The Governor, in his special message of January 9, 1872, says:

In the fall of 1868 I visited New-York City for the purpose of borrowing money on the credit of the State on coupon bonds, under the provisions of the acts of August 26, 1868. I had the assistance of Mr. H. H. Kimpton, United States Senator F. A. Sawyer, and Mr. George S. Cameron. I called at several of the most prominent banking-houses to effect the negotiation of the required loan, and they refused to advance any money upon our State securities, for those securities had been already branded with the threat of a speedy repudiation by the political opponents of the administration, who have ever since howled the same cry against the State credit. As the persons who made this threat controlled the press of the State, they were enabled to impress capitalists abroad with the false idea of a speedy reaction that would soon place them again in authority.

As the capitalists well knew that these persons, when in power in 1862, did repudiate their debts due Northern creditors, their distrust of our bonds was very natural and apparently well founded. It soon became evident to every man familiar with our financial standing in New York that, to negotiate the loan authorized, the question was not *what we would take for the bonds*, but *what we could get for them*. After much effort, and the most judicious management, I succeeded in borrowing money, through Mr. Cameron, at the rate of four dollars in bonds for one dollar in currency, the bonds being rated at seventy-five per cent. below their par value, or at twenty-five cents on the dollar. This loan, however, was only effected at the extravagant rate of one and a half per cent. per month, or eighteen per cent. a year —a rate only demanded on the most doubtful paper, to cover what is deemed a great risk—for the money loaned.

Subsequent loans were effected at a higher valuation of the bonds, but at rates of interest varying from fifteen to twenty per cent., in addition to commissions necessarily to be paid the financial agent. If, then, $3,200,000 in money have cost the State $9,514,000 in bonds, it does not, therefore, follow that the financial board have criminally conspired against the credit of the State, and, still less, that any *one member* of the board can justly be held up to public execration, or stigmatized by an accusation of "high crimes and misdemeanors," for the assumed results of its action. It is proper that I should add that the armed violence which has prevailed in this State for the past three years has had upon our bonds the same effect as actual war, in lessening their purchasing value, as money is dearer in war than in peace. Ku-kluxism made capitalists shrink from touching the bonds of this State, as a man would shrink from touching a pestilential body.

Those who complain of the low price at which our bonds have sold in the markets of the country, and that it has cost nine millions of bonds to buy less than three and

a half millions of dollars in currency, have only to examine
the testimony being developed before the United States
court, now in session in the capital of the State, to find an
easy solution for every financial evil that has afflicted the
people.

The committee add :

This may explain the increase of debt, and it is proba-
ble that money could not have been otherwise procured.
Yet we cannot agree that it was proper to submit to such
disastrous and degrading terms continually for three years.
Had the credit of the State been unsullied up to 1868, it
might have been expedient to make light loans on almost
any conditions to preserve her good name, or a great emergency might have justified such terms temporarily for
limited amounts; but for a State to go upon the "street"
as a mendicant borrower, and remain there buffeted from
broker to broker for three years, raising money to pay old
and dishonored debts at a cost of three dollars in renewed
obligations for every dollar paid, seems to us indefensible.
It is not justified by showing that it was legal, nor by the
fact that citizens of the State conspired to destroy her credit
in order to undermine the government.

The debt proper in 1871 is controverted. The documents before us tend to establish that the amount outstanding on the 20th day of December, 1871, was $15,768,-
306.27. This includes $3,773,000 bonds held as collateral
for a floating debt, alleged to be about $900,000. The old
bonded debt outstanding in 1868 was $6,454,306.27. Bonds
have since been issued and delivered to the financial agent
amounting to $9,514,000. Total, $15,968,306.27. There
are bonds held as sinking fund $200,000, which leaves bonds
outstanding $15,768,306.27. This includes $3,773,000 bonds
held as collateral for the floating debt, estimated at $900,-

000. It is claimed that these hypothecated bonds should be deducted and the floating debt added, which would make the debt $12,895,306.27. If the State were able to meet her obligations as they mature, there could be no reasonable objection to this deduction, but it is admitted that these bonds are pledged, on the street, in New-York City, at twenty-five cents on the dollar, to secure a floating debt nearly equal to their value at that rate; that the credit of the State is and has long been so depressed as to place her bonds at the mercy of usurers; that her financial agent has been accustomed, under authority of law, to pledge her securities at such rates; and that her bonds have been repeatedly sacrificed for want of means to redeem them. Hence we include these hypothecated bonds in our estimate of the debt.

There are bonds in the State Treasury, known as "the sterling loan," amounting to $6,000,000; of these, $3,500,000 have been executed, and $2,500,000 are unsigned. It is claimed that these bonds should be added to the outstanding debt. If the officials who have them in charge were men of acknowledged trustworthiness, such a claim would seem absurd. Certainly no financier would ask that bonds of the United States, printed but unsigned, or executed but unissued, in the vaults of the Treasury of the United States, the property of the Government, should be included in the national debt. But when officers of a State have concealed the truth and made false or grossly erroneous statements; when they have speculated on the expiring credit of the State, and grown rich while she has become bankrupt; when they are charged with corruption on probable proofs, and do not attempt, having opportunity, to meet the charges, prudent men may question the safety of funds in their hands. The risk is greater of executed than of unexecuted bonds, as a single officer might use the one, while

misapplication of the other would require concert. If the
$3,500,000 executed bonds were added, the amount would
be $19,268,306.27. If to this the $2,500,000 unexecuted
were added, the total would be $21,768,306.27. Having
presented the facts and alternate results, we deem it due the
State to say that, however well-grounded apprehensions as
to unissued bonds may be, they relate not to the past or the
present, but to the future; not to the amount of debt now,
or on any day past, but to what it may become; and before
allowing such fears to control our judgment, even as to the
future, we should consider the effect of recent and current
events in South Carolina.

Judge Carpenter, who testified before the
committee on the subject of the debt, says:

Question. What is your opinion of the amount of the
bonds of the State of South Carolina that have been hypothecated?

Answer. My opinion is, that all the bonds authorized
by the Legislature have been issued, and so far as I know
they have all either been sold or hypothecated. They are
as follows: By act of August 26, 1868, for redemption
of bills receivable, $500,000; by act of same date, for pay-
ment of interest on public debt, $1,000,000; by act of
September 15, 1868, for funding bills of Bank of the State
of South Carolina, $1,258,550—I see he puts it at more
than I thought; by act of February 17, 1869, for the relief of the Treasury, $1,000,000; by act of March 27, 1869,
for purposes of the Land Commission, $200,000; and by act
of March 1, 1870, for the same purpose, $500,000; making a
total of $4,458,550. I understand that to be the increase
of the State debt, so far as the bonded debt of the State is
concerned, since Governor Scott went into office; and
those bonds I understand to have been all sold or hy-

pothecated. In regard to the act for the relief of the
treasury, it is very peculiar in its phraseology; perhaps
not peculiar when taken in connection with certain statutes
of the United States, but peculiar in connection with the
statutes of South Carolina, or of any other State, so far as I
am apprised. The State collected that year over $1,100,000
in taxes from the people; a sum twice as great as it ever
cost before the war to run the entire machinery of the government of South Carolina, and more than twice as great as
it cost during Governor Orr's administration. After collect-
ing that sum of money, they then passed this act for the relief of the Treasury. The act was worded something in this
way: The Governor is authorized to borrow $1,000,000 for
the relief of the Treasury; and he was further authorized
to sell the bonds of the State for that purpose, at a price
to be fixed by him, the Controller-General, and the Treas-
urer-General, or to hypothecate them without any price
being fixed. Now, how many bonds have been issued under that act, which as you see may authorize him to issue
$2,000,000 instead of $1,000,000, I do not know, and
nobody but the Controller, the Treasurer, and the Governor does know. They admit that they have issued $1,-
000,000; how many more they have issued I do not know.

Question. But they may issue as many bonds as in
their judgment would produce to them $1,000,000.

Answer. Yes sir; they could issue any quantity of
bonds that by hypothecation would bring $1,000,000 into
the Treasury. The act authorized them to do that.

Question. Even though it might require $2,000,000
or $2,500,000 to produce that sum?

Answer. Just so. I think this statement is incorrect in
another respect; I do not think it states the debt on the
1st of October, 1867, as large as it was. It states it to be
$5,407,215.23. I think it was about $500,000 more

than that. I have made very careful investigations of this subject. It was some time ago, and it was then perfectly fresh in my mind. My conclusion, from the reports and every thing I could get hold of, was that the debt of the State was about $6,000,000 on the 1st of October, 1867. But, taking this statement of the Controller-General that the debt was then $5,407,215.23, then, in my judgment, there should be added to that the sum of $4,458,550 of bonds authorized by the Legislature to be issued by Governor Scott's administration; and then, in the next place, there should be added $4,000,000 of bonds guaranteed by the State to the Blue Ridge Railroad Company, and the mortgage for which was released by the last Legislature, and, in the third place, there should be added $2,000,000 of bonds in precisely the same condition in connection with the Greenville & Columbia Railroad.

Question. As this seems to be the proper place, state, as succinctly as you can, why that should be added as a debt, and whether it is not as certainly a debt as any portion of the funded debt.

Answer. Perhaps I had better go on with this statement, so that it can all be summed up together.

Question. Very well; go on and complete your statement as you desire.

Answer. Then there should be added about $1,000,-000—I am not certain as to the precise amount—of bonds to the Spartanburg & Union Railroad, and to the Laurensburg Railroad. The reason why I place in the list of debts of South Carolina the $2,000,000 of bonds indorsed for the Greenville & Columbia Railroad is, because the State, having heretofore held a mortgage upon that road, has released it, and the parties now owning the road have put a first mortgage upon it, and the road is in a bad condition, and could not be sold for enough to pay both amounts. In short, the State will never realize one cent out of that road; she has guaranteed the bonds, and she will have to pay them.

Question. In your judgment, the other mortgage, together with the cost of construction, will exhaust the road before the State will be reached?

Answer. I have no doubt of that. As to the Laurensburg branch, the State is a guarantor for some $375,000 or $400,000 of its bonds, with back interest now for eight or ten years; that road is already in the bankrupt court; has been decreed bankrupt by the Federal court, and has long since passed into the hands of a receiver.

Question. How about the $4,000,000 of the bonds of the Blue Ridge Railroad?

Answer. First, the Spartanburg road, in this connection: that is a bankrupt corporation, without being in bankruptcy, and utterly unable to pay its debt, and also with a large floating debt. The State can never be reached there, for the State has no lien on that road, or on the Laurensburg road. As to the Blue Ridge road, as I have already said, only twenty-nine miles of that road have been constructed. It will require $4,000,000 or $5,000,-000, in addition to the $4,000,000 guaranteed by the State, to build that road, and, until it is built, of course it can pay nothing. In other words, the bonds of the State were issued to take the place of original stock, and, through such a country as that, of course that stock would in any event all be sacrificed; and, if built with bonds instead of stock, they would be sacrificed. The State having given up its lien and allowed another mortgage to be put upon the road, if they go on with it they will be compelled to mortgage the road for as much as it would pay if sold.

Question. In fact, you regard that as an absolute debt of the State?

Answer. I regard the guaranteed bonds of that road, of the Greenville & Columbia road, of the Spartanburg road, and of the Laurensburg road, as so much debt of the State, as much so as any of the bonds issued by her.

Question. And none of them are embraced in this statement of the debt of the State?

Answer. Not one dollar of them. The State is guarantor for several other railroads which I have not enumerated, because I consider that they are able to pay, and will pay the debt themselves.

Question. These other liabilities in the aggregate amount to how much?

Answer. About $3,500,000 or $4,000,000.

Question. The State has to run the risk of any contingencies that may arise to depreciate the value of the property of those corporations; and, though you think she will be secure, it is not certain?

Answer. I regard those corporations as perfectly solvent and able to pay. I do not think the State is in any danger of being compelled to pay either the interest or the principal of those bonds.

Question. Can you form any thing like an estimate of what is the real amount that the State is now liable for?

Answer. By adding these figures together, in my opinion you can tell very quickly what is the debt of South Carolina, every dollar of which she will be compelled to pay. [Making a calculation.] It is about $17,450,000.

CHAPTER XIX.

On the Frauds practised in the Expenditure of $700,000, appropriated by the Legislature to buy Lands for the Freedmen.

AFTER Governor Scott's election in 1868, the subject of buying lands and dividing them up into small quantities, and distributing them among the blacks, was brought up for consideration. The purpose was humane and praiseworthy. In pursuance of it, a legislative appropriation was made in March, 1869, of $200,000, and in March, 1870, another of $500,000, making $700,000 in all.

The parties concerned in the application of the money, began at once to rob the State, and rob the freedmen of the advantages proposed by the appropriation. They bought land, worthless for the object in view, and, by collusion with the sellers, paid for it at a low price, and charged it to the State at a high one, thus swindling the State out of its appropriation, and the negroes out of the lands. The details of the transaction can be gathered from the extracts which follow.

Mr. Cardozo, the former Secretary of State,

and present State Treasurer, in his last annual report, speaks thus of the land-commission department:

In accordance with an act of the General Assembly, approved the 15th of February, 1872, abolishing the office of Land Commissioner, and devolving the duties of said office upon the Secretary of State, the Hon. H. E. Hayne, on the 1st of March following, delivered to me the records of the Land Commissioner's office, and I immediately assumed the duties of the same.

Mr. Hayne, during the short period of his occupancy of the office, though embarrassed by the want of funds, did much toward arranging the records of the office, bringing to the notice of your honorable body what his predecessors seemed to have made studied efforts to conceal—the disposition of the moneys appropriated for the purchase of land for the landless. But I found that much remained to be done, for, as yet, the persons for whose benefit the lands had been purchased had derived little or no benefit from them. Reports had reached me from reliable sources that many tracts of land were purchased at prices far above their actual value, and many who desired to purchase were unable and unwilling to pay two and three times the value of the land, notwithstanding the terms of sale were easy.

In order to acquaint myself with the true status of the case, the quality of the land, and the character of those who desired to purchase, I engaged the services of Mr. J. E. Green, sergeant-at-arms of the Senate, to visit each tract owned by the State, in person, and report to me the result of his investigations. Through the indefatigable energy of this gentleman, many hundreds of families have been provided with homes, and the Land Commission has been redeemed, in some measure at least, from the once truthful imputation of being an utter failure.

I was made a member of the Advisory Board when the law was passed in March, 1869. I most heartily sympathized with the object of the law, viz., to secure homes for the poor. I endeavored to discharge my duty faithfully as a member, but, on account of the conduct of the first Land Commissioner, C. P. Leslie, I resigned from the board in October, 1869, and would not cooperate with the board again until March 1, 1870, when Hon. R. C. De Large was appointed commissioner. It seemed almost impossible, however, for the beneficent enterprise which your honorable body originated to recover from the injuries which Mr. Leslie and his associates had inflicted upon it. I trust, however, it may still be the means of doing much good.

The accompanying table, from Mr. Cardozo's report, exhibits the details of the lands purchased, and discloses also an instance of discrepancy in the accounts, which is not an uncommon feature of South Carolina financial transactions. (*See* p. 153.)

It will be seen, by reference to the report of H. H. Kimpton, financial agent of the State (*see* Reports and Resolutions, 1871–'72, page 522), that he has paid, out of the Land Commission fund, upon drafts, etc., drawn on him by the State Treasurer, $712,71.19. It will also be seen, by reference to the reports of the Treasurer, that he has paid, on account of the Land Commission, $90,058.25, making a total expenditure, for the purposes of the Land Commission, of $802,137.44.

The total amount expended in the purchase of lands, as shown by the deeds on file in this office, is $577,517, leaving a difference of $224,620.44, which, so far as the records of this office show, is totally unaccounted for.

COUNTIES.	Total No. of Acres.	Total Cost.
Abbeville..............	2,742	$27,420 00
Anderson	645	2,945 00
Barnwell..............	842	3,310 00
Beaufort	3,375½	14,685 25
Charleston.............	25,501 6/10	106,962 50
Chester...............	1,251	10,373 00
Chesterfield...........	6,918	44,488 00
Clarendon.............	615	1,375 00
Colleton..............	12,894½	69,276 00
Darlington............	1,497½	11,603 75
Edgefield.............	2,778	18,823 00
Fairfield..............	4,124	23,344 00
Georgetown...........	6,023	21,085 00
Greenville............	1,776	14,115 00
Kershaw..............	6,360	29,510 00
Lancaster.............	1,204	8,032 00
Lexington.............	3,273	13,550 00
Marion................	6,661	25,480 00
Marlboro..............	800	10,000 00
Newberry.............	1,874	14,055 00
Oconee................	2,010	11,660 00
Orangeburg............	1,723½	5,000 00
Pickens...............	1,502	5,256 50
Richland..............	9,398	61,081 00
Spartanburg...........	1,972	12,567 00
Sumter................	454	2,000 00
Williamsburg..........	2,138	3,000 00
York	2,362	16,520 00
Totals..............	112,404 6/10	$577,517 00

According to my construction of the law, the whole appropriation of $700,000 should have been expended in the purchase of lands; and all expenses incurred for surveying, settling, etc., should have been paid out of the civil contingent fund of the State; and hence, whatever may have been the object for which the said sum of $224,-620.44 was used, other than the purchase of land, it has not been expended in accordance with the law of the Land Commission.

These lands were examined by an agency of the State Department, and the following are extracts from the reports :

BEAUFORT.

The Land Commission owns three tracts of land in this county. The first, the Rice Hope Tract, is very poor, the most of it being worn-out rice-fields. It is not yet settled. This land was bought at a most exorbitant price.

CHARLESTON.

The Land Commission owns over seventy-five thousand acres of land in this county, the most of it far remote from railway or water communication. It was with the greatest difficulty and at a large expense, that my agent was enabled to visit these lands and find out their quality, value, and adaptability for the purposes for which they have been purchased.

The Indian Grove Tract is situated in St. John's Berkley, and is divided into twenty-eight lots. A large portion of this land, known as the House Tract, is utterly worthless. The Wadboo Barony is poor, but little better than the former, five lots of which have been sold and settled.

The Cattle Bluff Tract was purchased from John Tuten, is situated on the Ashley River, in St. Andrew's Parish, and is divided into fourteen lots, thirteen of which have been settled. This land is also poor, and scarce of timber.

The Anendaw Tract (another of the Schley purchases) joins Wythewood on the north, and contains 12,800 acres.

The preliminary survey of this tract has been made, and 1,000 acres divided into lots for settlement. About 2,000 acres more are capable of cultivation; the balance is an interminable swamp, and utterly worthless.

CHESTERFIELD.

Columbia, S. C., *September* 14, 1872.
Hon. F. L. Cardozo, *Secretary of State.*

Sir: This is the report of the land of the State in Chesterfield County. It is thirty-three miles northeast of Cheraw. It is one vast sand-bed from one end to the other, and, if sold at one dollar per acre, no set of people under heaven could raise enough to pay for it.

J. E. GREEN, *Agent.*

This tract consists of 6,918 acres, and cost $44,418.

COLLETON.

Of a tract of 3,200 acres in the county of Colleton, it is said: "This land could not have been sold, *on time*, for fifty cents an acre. It was conveyed to the Land Commissioner for $19,500."

The Gilbert Plantation, purchased from L. D. Cummings, is situated six miles from Ross's Station on the South Carolina Railroad. The land is exceedingly poor; of fifty-three lots, but nine have been settled. It abounds in swamps, bays, and ponds, and is better for fishing than farming purposes.

The Four-Hole Tract, purchased from W. B. Brown, is very poor, overflowed, and worthless; not settled.

The McIntyre Tract, purchased from George F. McIntyre, is very poor; not settled.

PICKENS.

There are six tracts of land in this county, purchased by the State. They commence about three miles from

Pickens Court-House and run along Six Mile Creek. These lands are exceedingly poor, and no purchasers can be found at one dollar per acre. 1,502 acres, cost $5,256.50.

MARION.

The State purchased two tracts of land in Marion County. The Britton Neck Tract, purchased from J. H. Jenks, is situated forty miles from the Court-House, between the forks of the Pedee River. This tract is absolutely worthless, and will doubtless remain so until the river is drained by the ocean.

Of course, there were instances in which the commissioners were forced into proper purchases by the friends of the freedmen.

Of these we print two sample cases. One of these shows that, even where the land was good, there was a leak elsewhere :

EDGEFIELD.

The State purchased six tracts of land in this county. The quality of the land is excellent. The six tracts are divided into sixty-four lots, which are sold and settled. The State will realize from the sales of these lands fully as much as was paid for them. The people have paid their interest promptly. Mr. John Woolley, agent under Leslie, has received a large amount of money from these settlers, but has failed to turn it over to me, though repeatedly requested to do so.

CHARLESTON COUNTY.

The Rushland Plantation, sold to the State by C. T. Chase, is situated on John's Island. It is divided into forty-three lots, all of which have been settled. A more

thrifty and industrious set of farmers cannot be found in
the State. Several have settled in full for their lands, and
have their deeds for the same. Great credit is due to Miss
M. A. Sharp, a resident of the island, for the interest she
takes in these settlers, and, by her good advice and counsel,
many worthy people have secured homesteads for themselves and families.

Below is the testimony of Judge Carpenter
on this subject, taken by the committee of Congress:

Question. You say that $700,000 was appropriated by
the Legislature for the purchase of lands for the landless
and homes for the homeless. To what extent has that
$700,000 been expended, and how has it been applied?

Answer. Well, sir, I could not give a definite answer to
that question. I do not know how much of the money
was ever used for buying lands; a great deal of it certainly
has not been so used.

Question. What is your best information in regard to
that matter?

Answer. Judging by all that has been told me by the
persons in the different counties, and from my knowledge
of the workings of the Land Commission, I do not suppose
that the land that has been purchased by the State for the
$700,000 could be sold in the market to-day for more than
one-seventh of that amount, if it could be sold for that.
The Schley purchase, which was a large one, amounted to
$122,000; I think the tract of land consisted of about 30,-
000 acres, lying up the Ashley River, almost an entire, un-
broken swamp, utterly worthless except for the timber that
there is upon it; and, by any means that we have of cutting the timber and getting it out of the swamp, it is worth-

less for that purpose. There is a great deal of valuable timber upon it, if it could be got out, but, of course, without labor and capital, it cannot be got out. For the purpose for which it was purchased, it is utterly worthless. The land was offered in the North for months for $15,000, without finding a purchaser. There is not a county in the State where the Land Commission was not more or less swindled. At one time I had a statement of each county, and the precincts where the land was situated; the universal practice was for the local agent of the Land Commission to buy land at one price and put it into the Land Commission at another. The Rev. Mr. Donaldson, a State Senator from Chesterfield County, purchased a tract of land there; the excess of the amount for which he sold it over the amount for which he purchased it must have been between $20,000 and $30,000; I saw the tract of land and passed over it; it was worth very little.

Question. It was charged to the State for that much more than was paid for it?

Answer. Yes, sir. Another State Senator, Mr. Lunney, purchased a tract of land in Darlington County, and charged the State as much again as he gave. Indeed, I believe he took the money, and made no title to the State at that. During the latter part, the operations of the commission had got down to about this: When a man wanted to sell any land to the commission, he would charge three prices for it; one price he got himself, one price was taken by the go-between, and another price was taken by the Land Commission for themselves. That, I believe, is the way the thing wound up; I do not think it was as bad as that at first.

Question. It kept getting worse and worse as they learned how?

Answer. Yes, sir; or, as the fund grew less, they grew

more hungry. In other words, if you had a piece of land
that was worth $5,000, and you wanted to sell it to the
Land Commission, and I was the agent of the commission,
the arrangement would be for you to charge $15,000 for it,
of which you would take $5,000, I would take $5,000, and
the other $5,000 would go to the commissioners.

Question. You think the land would not realize one-
seventh of the amount appropriated by the Legislature for
that purpose?

Answer. I think more money was expended in the purchase of the land than $100,000; for I think that in a great
many instances it was a matter of personal favoritism to
give large prices for lands, and that they did so. But I do
not suppose that out of the $700,000 one hundred men in
South Carolina have got any land, and are living on it and
cultivating it to-day. Most of all the land is in the hands
of the State; most of the lands are unfit for cultivation;
either old worn-out lands, or else swampy new lands. It
has been a fruitful source of speculation and peculation, no
doubt about that; I do not think anybody doubts it; I
have never heard it denied by anybody; it was admitted on
all hands last summer, by Governor Scott's partisans and
friends, as well as by my friends, that there had been a
great deal of corruption and peculation in connection with
the expenditure of that fund.

Mr. Siebels, when asked to tell some of the
corrupt practices of the officials in South Carolina, said :

For instance, there is the appropriation for the land
commission; $700,000 was appropriated for buying lands
for the landless. It was intended that that money should
be expended in the purchase of land that was for sale

throughout the State; that the land was to be bought and paid for by the State authorities, and afterward sold in small quantities to the freedmen who had no land, on long credit. There was a land commissioner appointed, a Mr. C. P. Leslie, a man from New York. It was his duty to appoint sub-commissioners or agents in the several counties of the State, who were to purchase lands. All those purchases were to be submitted to an advisory board, of which Governor Scott was the chairman, and Attorney-General Chamberlain the legal adviser of the board, and of which the Secretary of State and the Treasurer of the State were to be members; the advisory board was to consist of five members. There never have been any books at all kept; there is no evidence of the amount of land that has been purchased; you cannot tell what has been bought, and you cannot tell what has been sold. We only know, after investigating and trying to find out what has been done, that land has been purchased as low as fifty cents an acre, and booked to the State at eight and ten dollars an acre; and in one single instance a tract of land near Charleston, which you will find on the map, called Hell-hole Swamp, was purchased at seventy-five cents an acre, or the whole tract for $26,100, and booked to the State at $120,000. One of the advisory board drew the money from the financial agent of the State in New York, a Mr. H. H. Kimpton.

Question. Which member of the advisory board?

Answer. It was said that the Treasurer of the State, Mr. Parker, did so. The facts were not denied; the accusation was openly made in our reform canvass; I made the accusation myself, in a public speech, and it was not denied.

By Mr. STEVENSON:

Question. Parker being the Treasurer of the State, he had power to draw the money?

Answer. Yes, sir.

By Mr. VAN TRUMP :

Question. What was the name of the Senator with whom you had that colloquy?

Answer. Beverly Nash.

By Mr. BECK :

Question. I want to ask you about two or three special cases. According to your information, how much of that $700,000 has been invested in good faith for homes for the negroes?

Answer. I was very diligent during the canvass in making inquiry, for we sought to use that as an electioneering document against them. I was very diligent in inquiring about the purchase of lands in all the counties, and I never heard of a single instance in which a *bona-fide* trade had been made.

Question. Your information is, that that $700,000 was substantially stolen by the officials?

Answer. Yes, sir; I do not believe that $100,000 of it was properly invested.

Mr. Suber, a leading lawyer of Newberry, South Carolina, when asked on these subjects, said :

Question. State your general information in regard to the management of the school fund, the land fund, railroad corporations, etc.

Answer. The Land Commission there has been the source of great complaint; it was created by an act of the Legislature with a view to buy lands for the landless and homes for the homeless, and $500,000 was first appropriated by the Legislature for that purpose. A man by the name of O. P. Leslie was appointed land commissioner for the State,

and charged with the duty of purchasing lands and resell-
ing them to indigent persons, in small lots of twenty-five,
forty, and fifty acres. Afterward $200,000 or $250,000
more was appropriated—$200,000, I think. All of that
money has been expended, and very few people have been
benefited by it. The general belief is, that a great deal
of corruption has been practised in that commission; for
instance, it is charged that bodies of land have been bought
by the commissioner at low figures, and charged to the
State at high figures in his accounts. There is one transaction in which it is said that a body of land lying in
Charleston District, entirely worthless, was bought for
$30,000, and charged up against the State for $120,000
That has been charged publicly, and it has not been denied by the parties who are said to have been guilty of it.

General Butler's attention was called to the
frauds practised by the Land Commission, and
the following resulted (pages 1207, 1208):

Question. You spoke of the fact that the owners were
considerably to blame also. Is it not a fact that the fraud
on the State, of the character to which you have referred,
buying at five dollars an acre and inserting in the deed a
consideration of ten dollars, could not have been consum-
mated without the cooperation of the venders?

Answer. Certainly, of course not.

Question. Were not the venders, in a very large degree,
the native South Carolinians here who owned the land?

Answer. Oh, yes, sir.

Question. So that, in reality, if the fraud exists to the
extent that is charged, they have at least given their countenance to it, whether they have profited by it or not?

Answer. Clearly so; and I think they are to blame for

it; but it was human nature almost. I do not think a strictly honest man would do it. If I had 10,000 acres of land to sell, and a Senator would come to me and say, "I will buy that if you will give me $500," I would buy him up as I would buy a mule.

On this subject, the legislative committee present the subjoined remarks. On page 14 they say :

THE LAND COMMISSION.—This gigantic folly, about which there has been more said, and less known, than any other branch of the State government, and of which the Legislature have often been challenged in open session to find out any thing about, as well as denied a report concerning its operations—this offspring of an ordinance of the Constitutional Convention, passed to furnish a certain individual with a visible occupation, and a more visible manipulation of the public funds—has, without doubt, been one of the most expensive experiments, productive of greater distress and dissatisfaction, that has been legalized or patronized by the State.

In no instance has the spirit of the ordinance alluded to, or the act authorizing the creation of the Land Commission, been carried out, as will be seen by the following extracts from both of these instruments ; but, on the other hand, the office, the administration of its power, the purchase of lands, the payment for the same, the sale of land-commission bonds, have all been made to subserve a certain organized result, viz., the primary benefit of members of the advisory board, and the land commissioners and their subservient allies.

In the examination of the books of the State Treasurer, or the vouchers to the charges made against the Land Commission, but little trace of the operations, and a small proportion of the amount expended by the commission, could be found. There seemed to be a studied silence on the whole subject; and, had the investigation ended with the Treasurer's or Controller's office, no more information would have been gained than was already given, viz., that less than $90,000 had been expended by the Land Commission at the close of the fiscal year ending October 31, 1870. Suspicions were aroused that a full record of all its transactions had not been made; and the subsequent examination of the books of the financial agent justified these suspicions; for in them it was found that, from the appointment of the first land commissioner to the 31st of October, 1870, according to the financial agent's charges, there had been paid out by him, in cash, for the Land Commission, $562,063.40, which, added to the amount, . . . swells the aggregate expended for and on account of the said Land Commission, as far as known, to $746,724.07.

The major part of the business transactions of the Land Commission was now performed by the financial agent in the city of New York, the accounts kept by him, as by a transcript of the same will be seen. To use the language of the financial agent, in answer to the question from the committee—"What has been the process by which the Land Commission transactions have been conducted between you as financial agent of the State of South Carolina and the State Treasurer?"—he says, "Instead of drawing on me, the Treasurer directed me to credit the State as having received the money from him, and charge the Land Commission with the same."

This plan, it will be apparent, obviated the necessity of charges upon the Treasurer's or even the land commissioner's books. As an illustration, in the case of the "Hell-hole Swamp" purchase, Parker gives drafts on H.

H. Kimpton, in favor of Z. B. Oakes, for $120,752. These are Kimpton's vouchers.

Parker pays the money at Columbia, the draft on Kimpton is the notice of the payment of money, the State is credited on Kimpton's books with the same amount in cash, and the Land Commission at the same time debited with the amount, and the whole transaction is safe, for details are not indulged in by the financial agent in his reports; nor do the advisory or financial board trouble the general assembly or the public with their suggestions or experience.

The statement will bear reiterating, that the Land Commission and its operations have been an "outrageous and enormous swindle," and the only satisfaction or comfort that the people of the State can take is, that, having expended more than the entire amount authorized by law, "the purposes of the land commission" have been gained, and no further expenditures can be made. That legal means to bring these fraudulent transactions to light, and the corrupt complicators to judgment, should be instituted and furthered there can be no division of sentiment upon; and the sooner the work is begun the less liable will the guilty be to cheat the demands of justice.

And Judge Poland speaks as follows:

A commission was organized to purchase lands for the purpose of furnishing homes, to the destitute laborers, at cheap rates and upon terms of easy payment, and $700,000 was appropriated for that purpose. The policy of the measure, in the then impoverished condition of the State, had its advocates and opponents in both Houses. The intention, if honestly carried out, was commendable; but the administration of the trust discloses, as already intimated by the extracts given, a greedy avidity by the owners of

land to sell; a willingness to insert in their deeds a price
higher than that they obtained—the difference to be used
as a corruption fund between themselves and the officers—
thus defrauding the State; making purchases of land unfit
for the purpose, at exorbitant prices, and defeating, in a
great degree, the benevolent purposes of the act.

Hon. J. E. Stevenson, in the following extract
from his report, seems impressed with the extraordinary value of these lands. Where his information comes from does not appear. We must
give him the benefit, however, of the acknowledgment that the report of the Secretary of State had
not then appeared. Mr. Stevenson says:

An act was passed March 27, 1869, and amended March
1, 1870, to establish a Land Commission, to purchase lands
to be sold as homesteads. Under these acts bonds were
issued, and are outstanding, amounting to $700,000, and
$547,329.85 have been expended, and 104,078 acres of land
have been purchased, at an average cost of $5.25 per acre,
which was probably below the intrinsic value, though
above the market price at which the same or better lands
might have been obtained when these were purchased.

No complaint has reached us of the policy of these acts,
and, if properly applied, it would have been beneficial to
the people and profitable to the State. But it is charged,
and the documents before us and evidence before the joint
committee tend to establish, that abuses were practised.
Lands were purchased not adapted to the purpose, fictitious prices charged the State, while owners received less,
and the difference was divided between the venders and
the officers or intermediates. The names of public officers
not connected with the commission, and of members of the

Legislature, appear in some sales. These practices have deprived the people of benefits and the State of a source of profit and prosperity, and brought the system into disrepute. The Governor recommends that the commission be abolished.

Governor Scott, speaking on this subject, in his special message of January 9, 1872, says (*see* pages 20 and 21):

Many of the purchases of land have been severely criticised, and, grave charges of irregularities in the administration of the office of land commissioner being current, I applied in the month of May, 1870, to an eminent lawyer of this city, Colonel J. D. Pope, to initiate legal proceedings for the purpose of bringing the alleged fraudulent transactions of the land commissioner under review in the courts. Colonel Pope stated, in a written opinion, which he furnished me, that, after a thorough investigation of the law and the facts in the premises, he was satisfied that great irregularities had been practised to the injury of the State, but that the necessary legal proofs of the malfeasance alleged could be furnished only by those who sold the lands, and by others interested in effecting such sales, and who profited by them, and they were not likely to appear as witnesses and criminate themselves.

CHAPTER XX.

THE State owned a quantity of the stock of the Columbia & Greenville road, and had a mortgage on the road, for advances in guarantees and certificates of indebtedness, to the amount of $2,000,000. This road fell into the hands of John Patterson, now Senator from South Carolina; Parker, the former State Treasurer, and Neagle, the former Controller of the State, and their confederates, by contrivances and methods described in the following statements. The upshot of which is, that the State lost its stock and lost its mortgage, which loss was the gain of those who became owners of the road. The value of the stock in the road owned by the State was estimated by the Controller, in 1869, at $433,000.

We have elsewhere referred to the Blue Ridge road as a corporation created to build a railroad into Kentucky and Tennessee across the southern end of the Blue Ridge, where it passes into South Carolina.

The enterprise has failed, and the company is bankrupt. The corporation has, however, been made useful as an engine to defraud the State. The company, in September, 1868, obtained a legislative guarantee of its bonds to the amount of $4,000,000, on certain conditions designed to protect the interests of the State.

By another legislative enactment in March, 1871, these conditions were all swept away, and the State left without any security, but with its full liability for the $4,000,000.

The statements and testimony which follow relate to these transactions.

But the case would be incomplete without the further statement that an issue of Blue Ridge Railroad scrip to the amount of $1,800,000 has since been authorized by the Legislature, and made available to the operators by declaring it receivable for taxes. This ingenious arrangement has afforded great opportunities for bargain and sale with the tax-collectors all over the State, who could buy the scrip of the operators at much less than its face, and turn it over to the Treasury at its par value.

The whole operation was clear profit on both sides, but at the expense of the immediate tax-payers, who must now be reassessed for the whole issue used in this way.

The scheme was found so profitable and so easily worked, that it is now alleged that two more fraudulent issues, each of the same amount, have been made, and thrown into circulation.

The Supreme Court, at its last session (February, 1873), declared the original issue fraudulent, but this decision cannot reach the operators in the fraud, who have of course taken care to unload themselves long ago. Neither will it relieve the tax-payers, whose money has been invested in the scrip.

In this way some fresh millions, as yet an unknown quantity, have been added to the debt, and added in such a way that the tax-payers cannot escape their speedy payment.

Part of the money gained by this operation has been since used to corrupt the Legislature in other cases, and to advance the personal and pecuniary objects of the authors of the fraud. The men who have done this have neither hanged themselves nor run away, but are to-day among the chief manipulators of South Carolina affairs, and the recipients of the honors of the State.

Judge Carpenter testifies before the congressional committee in this language :

The Legislature elected in that canvass then took their seats, and they proceeded at once to follow out the line of their predecessors. Bribery was the general order of the day to secure the passage of any thing. They had some very large jobs in relation to railroads that were carried out very much to the disgust of the people who have to pay the taxes, and who have any regard for public morality. The first Legislature passed an act guaranteeing $4,000,000 of bonds for the Blue Ridge Railroad, and reserving a statutory lien upon the road and its franchises, and its running stock, and every thing of the sort, for the payment of the $4,000,000. The same Legislature passed an act guaranteeing about $2,000,000 of bonds for the Greenville & Columbia Railroad, a road already running. Last winter the Legislature passed an act relieving both of these roads from their liability, so far as a mortgage was concerned, canceling the mortgage in favor of the State, and authorizing them to put a first-mortgage bond upon their road.

Question. Thus releasing the lien of the State?

Answer. Thus releasing the lien of the State entirely upon the two roads. Those two liens amount to about $6,000,000. The Blue Ridge Railroad had only about twenty-nine or thirty miles of road constructed. The estimates of the engineers are that it will require, in addition to the $4,000,000 guaranteed by the State, some $4,000,000 or $5,000,000 more to complete it. It runs through a mountainous country from Anderson, South Carolina, to Knoxville, Tennessee. That, of course, is assuming the debt by the State, for it is impossible that the road can pay it and finish the road. The State for two years has been paying the interest on the bonds of the road guaranteed by her, is doing so now, and has been doing so since the war, and I think she did so before. That has been the general character of the legislation of South Carolina.

Question. Who are the owners of the Greenville & Columbia Railroad, and of the Blue Ridge road, especially the first; in what way did they become the owners of it, and what legislation, if any, has been passed to aid them since they became the owners of the road?

Answer. In the case of the Blue Ridge road, to answer the shortest question first, the majority of the stock is owned by the State of South Carolina and the city of Charleston, and has been represented in the board of directors, in voting for officers, by Governor Scott and Mayor Pillsbury, the one Governor of the State, and the other Mayor of Charleston. There is very little stock outside of that, and they have managed it between them. I have stated the legislation in regard to the Blue Ridge road; first, the credit of the State—the indorsement of the State on its bonds to the amount of $4,000,000—and then the relinquishment of the mortgage held by the State. This is substantially all the legislation in regard to the Blue Ridge road, except one piece of legislation last winter, that I may more properly speak of in connection with the Greenville & Columbia road. The Greenville road is owned now by Colonel John Patterson, formerly of Pennsylvania; Governor Scott, whose stock, I think, is held by Joseph Crews, or his brother-in-law, Waterman, amounting, I think, and as I understand, to about three shares; by Parker, the State Treasurer; Neagle, the Controller of the State; and Cardozo, Secretary of State. I think Mr. Tomlinson has an interest in it. He was formerly Auditor of the State. I will not be sure of that, but he had an interest in it, and I think he has now. Timothy Hurley and others are also stockholders. I do not know all the present stockholders.

Question. Who is Timothy Hurley?

Answer. He is a member of the Legislature of South Carolina. Formerly he was a very active lobby member of the Legislature. The road was acquired by purchasing up in the country, through a portion of the directors of the Greenville & Columbia road, a certain amount of its stock, all that could be purchased in the up-country. That stock was transferred, in the first place, to three persons from Pennsylvania—Colonel McClure, Colonel Patterson, and a Mr. Taylor—under some arrangement with Governor Orr, who was one of the Board of Directors, Mr. Hammett, who was the president of the road, and Mr. Reed, who was the attorney of the road. A very considerable amount of the stock of the road was purchased in the country, and delivered to these parties. Then the parties divided the stock of the road into shares of $20,000 each; twelve shares, equal to $240,000. Then these different parties came in and subscribed one share, or half a share, or a quarter of a share, as they pleased, and took an interest in it in that way. That, however, did not give them a controlling amount of the stock of the road. They could not buy it in the market. It had got noised about, and there was a great deal of excitement about it. Then a bill was introduced in the Legislature in the interest of this ring, and it was passed. The bill authorized the Governor, the Controller, the Treasurer, the Attorney-General, the chairman of the Committee on Finance in the Senate, and the chairman of the Committee on Ways and Means in the House, to sell any of the public stocks or property held by the State of South Carolina, at public or private sale, with advertisement or without it, as they might deem proper. The object of the act was to enable them to sell to themselves the stock held by the State in the Greenville & Columbia road, probably some $300,000 or $400,000. That would give them a majority of the stock, and enable them to control the road. The bill was passed through the Legislature, as was asserted at the time, and never denied that I know of, by the usual means of procuring the passage of bills through that body. The stock was sold to some persons in New York, some friends of Mr. Kimpton. I do not know who they were. It was sold at $2.75 a share, the shares being

$50 each, when these same parties had been offering and paying for all the stock that could be brought to them from Newberry, as Colonel Fair informed me, $4 a share. They sold this stock to those men in New York, and it was afterward transferred to the different parties who held these several shares, and it is now owned by them.

Question. You spoke of aid being granted to that road by the Legislature. Was that done after they became the owners of the road?

Answer. No, sir; it was done before they became the owners of it. It was after that act that the mortgage was released.

Question. The mortgage of the State was released?

Answer. Yes, sir; after they became the owners of the road. That was this last winter, more than a year subsequent to the time when they acquired control of the stock of the road. Of course, other people own stock in the road who have never parted with it.

Question. That aid, granted by the State amounted to $2,000,000?

Answer. About $2,000,000. I believe the Controller-General states in his last report that under that act bonds to the amount of $1,500,000 have been issued. That is the only means I have of knowing how much has been issued; but the statute authorizes about $2,000,000.

Question. What consideration did the State receive from the Governor and his ring, as you call it, for the release of their first lien of $2,000,000?

Answer. The State received no consideration at all; what consideration the members of the Legislature received I am not able to say.

Question. The release operated to the extent of a grant or gift of $2,000,000 to the ring who controlled the road?

Answer. That is my opinion of it.

The report of the Republican State committee of investigation comments on this subject, and their report is quoted by the minority of the congressional committee. They say :

And in order to remove every obstacle to an immediate or entire use of these bonds which was restricted by conditions, under the act authorizing their issue, the fathers and abettors of the act of March, 1871, introduced section 6, which says: "The following clause in section 2 of the act of September 15, 1868, to authorize additional aid to the Blue Ridge Railroad Company in South Carolina, viz.: ' And further provided, that the said bonds, or any part thereof, shall not be used, unless upon the express condition that upon application to the Congress of the United States, or to private capitalists, the amount of $3,000,000 in currency, or so much of that sum as may be necessary, shall be furnished in exchange or upon the security of said bonds,' " is hereby repealed.

This repealing clause removes all hinderances to the use or negotiation of these bonds; and when it is borne in mind that so many of the State officers, financial board, and financial agent, were so much interested in " the promotion of the consolidation of the Greenville & Columbia and Blue Ridge Railroad Companies," and have the control and direction of these bonds, it is not too much to anticipate their advent upon " the market " when the emergency arises; hence they should have a permanent place among contingent if not actual liabilities.

And as the State has, by this same act, surrendered its prior lien upon the property, assets, effects, rights, and franchises of the Greenville & Columbia and Blue Ridge Railroad Companies, to be consolidated, and generously, before the marriage ceremony, advanced the bond-holders,

with their respective mortgage rights, to a first consideration in the settlement of claims, it will be expected that
the State will submit to a further use of its "faith and
funds," in order that the bond-holders may not suffer by
their investments. And further, as the 21,698 shares of
the State in the Greenville & Columbia Railroad Company,
which, in 1869, according to the Controller-General's
report, were valued at $433,960, have been sold, as per re-
port of Hon. J. H. Rainey, secretary of "the sinking-fund
commission," for $59,669.50, at the rate of $2.75 per share,
in order to put the management of the road into the
hands of the twelve associate consolidators and repealers,
there can be no contingency or fortuitous circumstance
which will prevent the putting upon "the market" of
every bond issued and indorsed, authorized by statutory
provisions.

The report of the Tax-payers' Convention, held
in Columbia, refers to those transactions in the
following terms :

But the Greenville & Columbia Railroad Company also
has a history. Certain men, well known to this convention, acting as agents for a ring of speculators, had by de-
ception and misrepresentation purchased the stock held by
private individuals at a nominal price. The Governor, by
authority of the Legislature, then sold the State stock in
this company to the same "ring," in which high State
officials are the chief jewels. I have authority for saying
that money to make these purchases was raised by hy-
pothecating State bonds. So, then, the corporation known
as the Greenville & Columbia Railroad Company passed
into the hands of private individuals who never paid out
of their own pockets one cent for the stock, and became,

what it yet is, a disreputable ring of State officials, and bankrupt stock-jobbers.

And again :

That, upon a careful examination of the act of the Legislature, we can reach but one conclusion : That, for some reasons unknown to your committee, the Legislature has, without consideration, relinquished to private individuals the State's lien upon the Blue Ridge Railroad, and the entire properties of the other companies (styled companies in the act), the Greenville & Columbia Railroad Company. Such dealings by trustees with the property or funds of their *cestui que* trust, can only be the result of fraud, are unauthorized by law, and are void.

Major Harley, of that convention, speaks as follows :

It is known, Mr. President, that, during the session of the last Legislature, measures were introduced into both Houses, looking to the benefit of the Greenville & Columbia Railroad ring (for it had ceased to be a company), and at the same time to the destruction of the Blue Ridge Railroad Company. I desire, in this connection, to refer more particularly to Mr. Whittemore's bill to withdraw the indorsement of the State from the bonds of the Blue Ridge Railroad Company to the amount of $4,000,000. The passage of this bill would have been a death-blow to this company. It may be, and it probably is, the truth that, to save itself, this company associated with that mass of corruption, the Greenville & Columbia Railroad ring, the instigator and principal agent in the stupendous fraud which resulted from the association. Am I to be told that under such circumstances the managers and officers of the Blue Ridge Company were justified in resorting to deception, bribery, and fraud? This may furnish a reason; but it supplies no excuse.

To accomplish this end, to consummate this scheme of fraud and villainy, they concoct the extraordinary act of Assembly which has provoked this investigation. Gentlemen of the convention, some of you have been familiar with legislation in South Carolina for many years; I see around me some who legislated for the commonwealth in connection with Cheves, Hayne, McDuffie, Calhoun, and a host of others, whose names are household words about our desolated fireplaces of to-day; I say to you, read this act, and I venture to say, with your long experience, you will pronounce it the most remarkable piece of legislation ever brought to your attention. The two corporations go before the Legislature, and represent the great advantage and the many blessings which will result to the State, as the consequence of their consolidation; and they ask the Legislature, in view of the many public advantages to result therefrom, to grant them certain favors. What they wished I have already stated. Just allow me to add here, that their modest request involved the subordination, by the State, of her first lien upon their respective roads, for amounts exceeding $6,000,000 to the junior claims of private persons. This act is prepared, passed, and ratified. All that these corporations ask for is given; not, however, upon the consolidation being actually effected; but, to use the words of the act, "in view" of the proposed consolidation, these great favors are granted by legislative enactment.

Mr. President, one prominent feature in this transaction is the part which native Carolinians have played in it; and it is to this feature that I ask to be allowed to address myself in closing. I say, sir, and I say it in sorrow, that some of our own household, men whom the State in the past has delighted to honor, but whose honors have been withered by the atmosphere of corruption that they breathe, are involved in this swindle. I cannot conceive how these men, thoroughly acquainted as they are with the negro character, and with the circumstances which, up to a recent date, surrounded the negroes then in slavery—knowing, as they well know, that in mature manhood the negro is mentally a child, and that, morally, he never passes the stature of infancy, could reconcile it to themselves to approach them, when by force of law they were suddenly raised to political power, and, by appealing to their cupidity and avarice, make them their instruments to effect the robbery of their impoverished white brethren. The highwayman spares the idiot, the pirate has mercy on the fool; but these, our own people, use idiot and fool alike to consummate their schemes of spoliation and plunder. A Legislature, composed chiefly of our former slaves, has been bribed by these men—to do what? To give them the privilege, by law, of plundering the property-holders of the State, now almost bankrupt, by reason of the burden of taxation under which they labor.

CHAPTER XXI.

On the Frauds and Violence practised in the Elections.

ONE of the great discouragements to regular and sustained efforts on the part of the whites to resist negro sway in South Carolina, has been the frauds practised on the ballot-box. These have been so great and so audacious, that voting became a farce. The party in the majority counted in whomever they wanted elected, without any reference to the votes cast.

The following testimony discloses a worse state of things in South Carolina on this subject, than was ever before seen since voting was invented. It shows that men who were elected by a majority of thousands, were deliberately counted out, and their adversaries declared elected by overwhelming majorities. The result has been, that at the last election no voting was done in numerous districts except by the dominant party in the State.

Referring to this subject, Judge Poland, in his report, says:

The election law of the State is one which could not be better calculated to produce frauds by affording the facilities to commit and conceal them, and, tempted by these facilities, we cannot doubt that in many instances they were committed.

Mr. Van Trump, of the congressional committee, reports as follows:

On the 16th day of March, 1869, there was passed, and approved by the Executive, an act entitled "An act to organize and govern the militia of the State of South Carolina." It is in form a general law, and, of course, to be valid, must apply to all the citizens of the Commonwealth of the prescribed age, white as well as black. But the design of the law itself will be best exhibited by the improper use made of it during the summer of the next year after its passage, which, as contemplated in its enactment, was made to control the election of that year, the Governor himself being a candidate for reëlection. The following is the fourteenth section of the law:

SEC. 14. That the organized militia of this State shall be known as the National Guard of the State of South Carolina, and shall consist of such divisions, brigades, regiments, and battalions, and, in addition thereto, such batteries of artillery, and troops and squadrons of cavalry, as the commander-in-chief may deem expedient; and nothing herein contained shall be so construed as to interfere with the power of the commander-in-chief, in case of war or insurrection, or of imminent danger thereof, to order drafts of the militia, and to form new regiments, battalions, brigades, or divisions, as he may deem just and proper: *Provided*, That there shall be no military organizations or formations for the purpose of arming, drilling, exercising the

manual of arms, or military manœuvres, not authorized by
this act and by the commander-in-chief; and any neglect
or violations of the provisions of this section shall, upon
conviction, be punished with imprisonment at hard labor
in the State penitentiary for a term not less than one year,
nor more than three years, at the discretion of a competent court.

The statute was permitted to lie dormant until the
spring of 1870. At that period, the corruptions of the
State government, in all its various departments, had so
culminated and become known to the people, that an attempt was made to unite the elements of opposition in what
is known as the "reform" movement. It was thought,
though, as events proved, mistakenly, that if a mixed ticket
of Conservatives and dissatisfied Republicans were put in
the field, there might be some chance. Such a ticket was
made up at an early day, and the organization assumed the
name of the "reform party," with Judge Carpenter, a Republican, at its head, as a candidate against Scott for Governor. Scott sent through the State to enroll and organize
the negro population, and fourteen full regiments were thus
organized in the several counties of the State.

In regard to the election itself the testimony
is subjoined.

Mr. Corbin, the United States District Attorney for South Carolina, a Republican, testifies as
follows :

Question. What is the machinery of election there?

Answer. At the last election it was a very miserable
machinery. Do you wish me to state the details of the
law ?

Question. Yes, sir.

Answer. The last Legislature but one passed a general law.

Mr. Poland. Is there not a shorter way to get at the law than by asking the witness to state his recollection of it?

Mr. Blair. I would like to hear from the witness how it worked.

The Witness. The machinery was briefly this: three commissioners were appointed for each county by the Governor; those three commissioners appointed managers in the several precincts in the county, and were to furnish those managers with ballot-boxes locked and sealed, except an aperture through which to deposit the votes in the box. The managers were to receive the votes on the day of election, keep a poll-list, and return the poll-list and the box to the commissioners of election, who were to count the votes; they were to do that within three days after the election; they had three days within which to return the boxes and poll-lists.

By Mr. Blair:

Question. To the commissioners?

Answer. Yes, sir; and then the commissioners were required by law, within ten days, to canvass the vote and make return to the State board of canvassers; and the State board was to canvass the result and declare it.

Question. General Scott, the Governor, who had the appointment of the commissioners, was himself a candidate for reëlection as Governor, was he not?

Answer. Certainly.

Question. Therefore he had it in his power to appoint every person who had any thing in the State to do with receiving and counting the votes?

Answer. All but the managers; he appointed the commissioners only.

Question. Well, the commissioners appointed the managers?

Answer. Certainly.

Question. Therefore he had the control, directly or indirectly, of every person in the State who had any thing to do with counting the votes by which he was to be either reelected or defeated? I understand that to be the state of the case?

Answer. Yes, sir; there is no doubt about it. But the great difficulty under that election law and the working of it arose simply from the dishonesty of the managers or commissioners; that is, where the frauds were committed, if they were committed at all.

Question. Did not the law itself contemplate that very thing; does it not give the opportunity?

Answer. Of course, every one in office has the opportunity to commit rascalities and frauds. If every officer had been honest the election returns would have been as correct under that law as under any law. Still, you can see what the opportunities were; the managers had the boxes at their precincts, remote from the county-seat, and, having received the votes, they sealed up their boxes as they were required. Some of them had to carry them thirty and forty and fifty miles to the county-seat, to deliver them to the commissioners. If they chose to knock out the bottom and put in other votes, or to change those that were in there, they had the opportunity to do it. And, after the boxes were received by the commissioners, they had the same opportunity to commit frauds, because the boxes were in their custody for ten days. Some very glaring frauds were doubtless committed in some of the lower counties. At the very last term of the court I convicted three parties in Beaufort County for abstracting ballots that had been cast by the voters at the election and substituting others for them, and also for erasing the names of some of the candidates upon the ballots cast and substituting others therefor. After a very deliberate trial, that extended over three weeks, the first trial resulted in a mistrial; but on the second trial we convicted them on all the counts against them.

Mr. E. W. Siebels, of Columbia, when before the committee, testified as follows:

Question. Was there not a large amount of fraud practised in your State at the last election?

Answer. Yes, sir; some voting a dozen times, perhaps; women and children voted. Women gave votes for their husbands or their brothers, who they said were sick. After we elected a few members, they voted them right square out of the Legislature. We elected some of our candidates by a hundred-and-odd majority; yet the Legislature declared their seats vacant. They did every thing according to their own account. These are facts which are on record. I think many of these facts were developed in the Bowen and De Large controversy that has been going on in Charleston. Yes, sir; boxes were opened and votes were changed. They committed fraud in a dozen different ways. I know a gentleman whose uncle voted for him, and they found the ticket on which his uncle had written his name, in his own handwriting, and they had afterward scratched it out. I am certain that, if we had had any election at all, we would have elected the members of the Reform party, or the Democratic party, in fourteen counties, perhaps in more. We thought we stood a good chance in sixteen counties out of the thirty-one.

Judge Carpenter testified to the following effect:

Question. I believe you have stated that the negroes who desired to vote for you, or for the Reform ticket, were maltreated, threatened, and persecuted by their colored brethren. Was that general throughout the State?

Answer. I think it was. I was told so in every county that I was in, by more than one colored man. As I said before, I heard men proclaim that the order had been issued to shoot any colored man who voted for the Reform ticket. I do not think there was any such order, but that was the statement.

Question. Was it believed by those people?

Answer. Undoubtedly it was believed by the colored people.

Question. And acted upon?

Answer. And acted upon.

Question. Were the election managers so divided as to give you any chance in the counting of votes, or were they generally friends of Governor Scott?

Answer. They were all friends of Governor Scott, without any exception, so far as I know; that is, the commissioners of election; and the managers were his friends without any exception, except where nobody was found that was able to read and write of their party, and then they had to resort to the reformers for managers. Once in a while there would be a precinct where no colored man could read and write, and then they had to take a reformer to take down the names on the poll-list.

Question. As a matter of necessity?

Answer. Yes, sir. I do not think there was any reformer in the State appointed, as commissioner or manager, other than from necessity.

Question. If in these elections the frauds were as great as you supposed they were, what was the obstacle under the laws of the State to exposing them and making contest?

Answer. There was no penalty affixed to the law of the State for any offense connected with the election. The only way to prosecute them was in the United States courts, under the Federal statutes.

Question. Under the statute known as the enforcement bill?

Answer. Yes, sir; that was the statute under which those men in Beaufort County were prosecuted; but then it was so difficult to obtain the proof. The act of the Legislature did not require the managers to keep the ballots at all, and they did not keep them. They certified that A B had so many votes for Congress, that C D had so many, that E F had so many votes for Governor, and so on, and then they destroyed the ballots. They did not leave any thing by which to trace them. The way those persons were convicted in Beaufort was by bringing men from the precincts to swear how they had voted. To illustrate the whole thing, in one precinct where the commissioners returned but six votes as having been given for a certain party, forty-one men were brought forward who swore they voted for that party; and so it was in other precincts. That showed that the commissioner had taken ballots from the boxes, and put others in their stead. The act, if you can call it one—I call it a device—was so framed as to enable them to destroy any trace of their guilt in the matter. The only thing that could be relied upon was the general statement of the certificate of the commissioners, who, as I said a while ago, were themselves almost universally candidates for office.

Question. The party in power could have been maintained under that law, no matter what majority the people might cast against it?

Answer. If there had been forty thousand majority, there would not have been any difference; it would have been just the same, for the law was framed for that purpose.

Question. You spoke of the district of Mr. Wallace as an illustration. What facts have you to satisfy you that in his district the count was false?

Answer. I canvassed that district very thoroughly; I canvassed it almost by precincts. In the first place it has a large preponderance of white votes.

Question. Where does the district lay?

Answer. It is Chester, York, and Laurens, and in that region of the State. I talked with a great number of persons, intelligent men of both parties; I obtained information from both sides as to the particular counties. I talked with colored men throughout the entire district, and I made up my mind that the majority for General McKissick in that district would be about six or seven thousand. It was owing to two facts that I came to this conclusion. First, the character of the population, and second, the very active and thorough canvass of the whole district, without the exception of a county. I never saw any one during the campaign, black or white, that had any idea that Wallace was going to be elected, and I do not think that any one was more astonished than his own partisans when they found that he had three or four thousand majority in that district. He had just been beaten by about five thousand majority by Simpson. Simpson was disqualified, and Wallace was therefore given the seat. He ran this race with McKissick, who is a very popular stumper, and a popular man in that region of country; besides, there is a great deal of dissatisfaction toward Wallace among his own people. But it was a part of the general scheme to keep power in the hands of the officials of the State, no matter how the people voted.

Question. How much of joint debate had you in the canvass?

Answer. Very little; no debate at all with Governor Scott. I think I had about four general discussions, at different places, with candidates of the other side for State offices and candidates for Congress; but none with Governor Scott, for he did not make his appearance on the stump at all. In the fourth congressional district, represented in your House by Mr. Wallace, the commissioners' returns make him elected by some three or four thousand majority, I think. Now, judging from a very active and thorough canvass of the whole country, and from information of men of all parties generally, I do not think he could have been beaten there by less than six or seven thousand votes. In the county of Chesterfield, where the white population largely predominates, where the Reform Senator was elected by a handsome majority, the commissioners returned to the Lower House two members as elected who were friends of Governor Scott, and the House seated them. I think it was universal with the Republican papers in the State that they denounced it as an outrage; these men never could and never did have a majority. The *Charleston Republican* and the Republican paper of Columbia both very severely denounced the action of the House, particularly the *Charleston Republican*. I do not pretend to state what the opinion of the people was as to the real result of the canvass; but it was the general opinion throughout the State, after the election, that the ballot-boxes had been tampered with throughout the State, and the will of the people entirely disregarded. In Laurens, where Crews was a commissioner and also a candidate for the Legislature at the same time the other two commissioners were, one, a man by the name of Owens, and a Senator, a very weak man, perfectly under the dominion of Crews, and the other a negro, also under his dominion: they returned a thousand majority in that county for Scott and Wallace. I am as certain that I received a thousand majority in that county as I am of my existence.

Question. How was the vote against you returned?

Answer. It was a round thousand against everybody on our ticket, and a thousand in favor of everybody on the other ticket. I do not think they ever counted the ballots.

CHAPTER XXII.

The Frauds in relation to the Redemption of the Notes of the Bank of South Carolina.

THE State of South Carolina was bound to redeem, by an obligation antedating the war, certain outstanding circulating notes of the State Bank.

The amount of these notes was not known. A suit had been commenced after the war, and holders of these bills had been, by an order of court, notified to present them. At the end of a year and a half of the widest publicity of the order, the holders had been able to find and present to the court something less than half a million of the notes. This amount was and is supposed to have been the sum total of the then existing issue.

At this point the Legislature took up the case and voted to issue State bonds to redeem them. The first step was to appoint a legislative committee to count them. To the astonishment of everybody that committee reported to the House that they had attended to their duty, and found

$1,258,550 in notes, as the result of their endeavors.

By means of the customary persuasions, the Legislature were induced to overlook the fact that less than $500,000 could be found previously to be extant, after eighteen months' vigorous search; and passed an act authorizing an emission of bonds to the amount of the $1,258,550.

The next step in the transaction was by the Executive Department, which had printed and issued bonds for this specific purpose, expressed on their face, for the sum of $1,590,000.

By this one simple operation, the State thus appears to have been defrauded of a round million.

The case is explained in detail in the following testimony of Judge Carpenter:

Question. Have you any information as to who were the principal owners of the notes of the Bank of the State of South Carolina to the amount of twelve hundred and odd thousand dollars, which is referred to in the statement of the Controller-General? Do you know how that affair was managed, and how those notes were obtained and paid off?

Answer. I know something about them. I think that perhaps the largest holder of the notes was Edwin Parsons, of New York; perhaps the next largest holder was a man by the name of Marsh, from Cincinnati, Ohio; and Governor Scott was a very considerable holder of these bills. I think most of the gentlemen composing the State government were interested in them, as well as several members of the Legislature. I think Governor Scott had probably some

$60,000 or $70,000; I am not certain as to the amount. He told me at one time that he had $50,000, and I know that he afterward purchased more. I think that most of those who are called the ring there had an interest in them; if they did not have the bills themselves, they had an interest in the bonds after the bills were funded.

Question. How was that funding accomplished?

Answer. Well, by an act of the Legislature. I do not think they got much for passing that; it was in the early days, and they were green about such things. I have heard some parties say that they got along very well with that. Those fellows had not learned their business well when that bill was passed. I think it was got through without a great deal of money, very little money indeed; but I think a great many more bonds were issued than there were bills filed. I think the speculation there was in that way principally. It was asserted—well, there was a suit by Dabney, Morgan & Co., plaintiffs, against the Bank of the State, in the name of a bill against an insolvent debtor. That suit was referred to a master in equity, to take proof as to the outstanding bills of the bank, and the holders of those bills were required to come in and present them and prove them. In that case there was proved something less than $500,000 of the bills. The case had been in court a year and a half or more; had been a very prominent case; was widely known; and there was something less than half a million of the bills there proved. Those bills were withdrawn from that court by leave of the court. To the astonishment of everybody who had been familiar with the affairs of the State, when the bonds came to be issued for the funding of those bills, they footed up between $1,200,000 and $1,300,000, instead of what everybody supposed would be the case, between $600,000 and $700,000. One of the committee to count the bills was

Mr. Joseph Crews, of Laurens; another of the committee
was a Mr. Rainey, now a member of your House; and the
third was the Treasurer of the State, I believe, Mr. Parker. After these bonds had been issued, shortly afterward,
it seems that Mr. Crews deposited with Scott, Williams &
Co., $30,000 of these bills. Nobody knew any thing about
it until last year, when Scott, Williams & Co. sued Crews
for some money he owed them. Then this state of facts
was disclosed on the trial: Scott, Williams & Co.'s bank
had been robbed before the institution of the suit against
Crews, and among other property taken by the robbers
was this $30,000 of the bills of the Bank of the State of
South Carolina. It turned out that shortly after the bills
were counted and supposed to have been destroyed, Crews
had deposited this amount as collateral security for money
that he had borrowed of that bank. In the suit he insisted
that he ought not to pay the amount he had borrowed, because the bank had allowed the collateral security to be
stolen.

Question. This $30,000 was supposed to be part of the
bills understood to have been destroyed by the committee
of which Crews was a member?

Answer. It was supposed they were all destroyed.
Where he got this $30,000, when it was supposed that all
these bills had been counted and destroyed, of course I do
not know. He was one of the committee that counted
them.

The case is handled thus gently by Hon. J. E.
Stevenson:

There were outstanding, when the new government
came in, notes of the Bank of South Carolina, which the
State was bound to redeem, $1,258,550, with interest; and
an act was passed September 15, 1868, for the redemption

of these notes, under which bonds were issued, $1,590,000, of which, $1,259,000 are outstanding, and $331,000 are in the Treasury. Members of both parties voted for this measure, which appeared to be one of justice to public creditors; but it is now alleged, and there is evidence before the joint committee to sustain the charge, that notes had been purchased at nominal rates, and were held in large quantities by State officers, members of the Legislature, and influential citizens of both parties, and that the act enabled them to make a speculation on the credit of the State.

It has also been charged that the notes redeemed were not destroyed, but the documents before us refute this charge.

The legislative committee, in their report, say:

Since the foregoing was written it is found that, of the bonds to redeem bills of the Bank of the State of South Carolina, $1,250,000 were sent by the American Bank Note Company to the State Treasurer, and $340,000 to the Governor. In whose hands, then, the balance of the said bonds, viz., $331,450, may be found is not yet known to the committee.

How many bills of the Bank of the State had been presented to the Treasurer up to January 1, 1869, or bonds issued for their payment, is not known, but $500,000 of the bonds classed as " Loan to redeem bills of the Bank of the State of South Carolina," had been printed; and before the adjournment of the session of the General Assembly of 1868 and 1869, $1,075,000 more of the same bonds had been printed. After the adjournment of the General Assembly in April, 1869, $15,000 more were printed, making in the aggregate $1,590,000.

The excess printed over the amount issued, in whomsoever hands they may be found, should be at once canceled or destroyed, as the legal time for the presentation and conversion of the bills of the Bank of the State has already passed, and no further issue has been authorized.

CHAPTER XXIII.

The Census Frauds.

THE minority of the joint committee of Congress report two of the minor transactions of the Legislature, by way of showing their liberality and ingenuity in disposing of the State's money.

The first was an appropriation to take a census of the State in 1869, just previous to the regular national census of 1870, for which they paid $75,000; and the second was by the same body, to pay the Speaker $1,000, by way of gratuity, to reimburse his losses on a horse-race.

We give the account of both transactions in the language of the committee. It is given as an illustration of the free-and-easy way of doing things that prevails in that quarter.

They say:

The report of the "joint special financial investigating committee," made at the last session of the Legislature, shows the following disbursements for taking a State census, in 1869–'70, only a few months before the Federal census:

June, 1869	$120
July, 1869..	4,231
August, 1869....................................	8,851
September, 1869.................................	17,180
October, 1869	19,746
November, 1869.................................	12,165
December, 1869	5,189
January, 1870....................................	6,170
February, 1870	1,472
March, 1870	56
April, 1870......................................	148
May, 1870..	196
Total...................................	$75,524

The State census-takers had scarcely retired from the field of their operations before the advent of the Federal officers occurred to do the same thing. The first act of the State Legislature for taking the census was passed and approved March 19, 1869, which required the work to be completed by the 1st day of November, 1869. On the 18th of December, 1869, an amendatory act was passed, extending the time for the completion of the work to December 31, 1869. The Federal census bill was introduced into Congress on the 6th of December, 1869, and finally passed both Houses on the 4th day of May, 1870, and the work commenced on the 1st day of June, 1870; so that it will be observed that legislation to do the same thing was pending at the same time in Congress and the Legislature of South Carolina.

The taking of the Federal census, under the late law of Congress passed for that purpose, was a much more laborious and expensive one, for the reason that it required a detailed statement of the statistics, social, commercial, and agricultural, of each State of the Union, to be carefully made up as a part of the census record.

The following communication, furnished us by the Census Bureau, exhibits the difference in the amount expended on the two enumerations:

DEPARTMENT OF THE INTERIOR, }
WASHINGTON, D. C., *February* 5, 1872. }

SIR: The total expense of taking the census in the State of South Carolina, as appears on the books of this office, amounted to $43,203.13. This, of course, does not include the expense of compilation, tabulation, etc., in the census-office—only the actual cost of taking and making return of the census.

Very respectfully, yours, etc.,

HENRY STONE,
Acting Chief Clerk.

Hon. P. VAN TRUMP,
House of Representatives.

The journals of the last session of the Legislature show that a joint resolution was adopted to adjourn on the 7th day of March last. The proceedings, for several weeks prior to that time, show great activity and industry in the passage of private bills, to get through by the day fixed for adjournment. In the House, particularly, this was so, holding frequent night sessions as late as the hour of midnight. The journal of the House shows that on the 4th day of March, only three days prior to the final adjournment, the House took a recess from ten o'clock in the morning to seven in the evening.

One F. I. Moses, Jr., from Brooklyn, New York, was the Speaker of the House. There was a negro member of the House by the name of Whipper, who was the proprietor of fast horses. Moses and Whipper had made up a match-race for $1,000 a side. The race was fixed to come off on the said 4th day of March; and the explanation of the recess on that day is, that the House adjourned to attend this horse-race. The race was run; and the Speaker lost the bet of $1,000. Three days afterward, on the day of final adjournment, and the very last thing done in the House, as shown by the journal, was a motion made by Whipper, "that a gratuity of $1,000 be voted to the Speaker of this House, for the dignity and ability with which he has presided over its deliberations." The motion was passed by a large majority.

CHAPTER XXIV.

Frauds in furnishing State-House.

THE following testimony relates to a piece of extravagance of expenditure in fitting up the legislative halls, and of frauds in connection with it, in which an implicated member defies exposure, and threatens to enlarge penitentiary accommodations for the members, in the event of his own discomfiture.

The testimony was taken before the joint committee of Congress, and is appended:

Question. Was there, or not, an order at the last session of the Legislature, for the furnishing of the House of Representatives, and a bill produced there by the chairman of the committee appointed to do it?

Answer. Yes, sir.

Question. State who he was, what was the amount of the bill produced, and what was done in regard to it.

Answer. At the session before the last there was a resolution passed the House, that a committee be appointed to purchase furniture for the House of Representatives; the Senate had been finished and furnished before. This committee was appointed, and Mr. John B. Dennis was the chairman of it. When the Legislature met the last time the new furniture was all in; the House was furnished most superbly. A great deal was said in the papers about the extravagance; a great deal of talk was made about the carpets being so fine and about the magnificent chandeliers and spittoons, and one thing and another, for an impoverished people. Even several Republicans said to me that it provoked them to see so much extravagance, when we were so little able to afford it. It was a theme of conversation with everybody. When the bill came in it amounted to $95,000. That created a terrible excitement in the House. We had only twenty-three members in the House, I believe; some of them moved that the bill be printed, but they would not print that bill. One of the members said it would cost $2,000 to print the bill, and that they had better not print it. They staved it off until the very last day of the session. When they had spent $200,000 or $300,000 in the way of expenditures, they brought in another bill for two hundred and odd thousand dollars on the very last day of the session, out of which this $95,000 was to be paid. But the Governor, who had taken a very decided stand in regard to the reckless expenditure of the public money, swore that that bill never should be paid. He vetoed the bill, and the Senate sustained the veto. Since then some gentlemen, interested to see what on earth this bill could be for, how the things could cost so much, because there were the goods to show for themselves, ferreted the matter out. And, although the highest prices were paid for this furniture, three or four or five times its value—for instance, $750 was paid for one mirror in the Speaker's room; each official has a separate room for himself, most gorgeously fitted up, with toilet sets and all the paraphernalia of a dwelling-house; clocks, at $480 apiece; chandeliers, at $650—

Question. How many spittoons were there?

Answer. There were two hundred fine porcelain spittoons, at eight dollars apiece.

Question. There were only one hundred and twenty-four members?

Answer. Yes, sir.

Question. What were the bills really found to foot up?

Answer. The bills were obtained and sent to Columbia, and we had them published in all the papers. They foot up to fifty and some odd thousand dollars; I have the bills myself.

By Mr. VAN TRUMP:

Question. So that reduced the bill about $40,000 below what it was first put at by the committee?

Answer. They never reduced it at all.

By Mr. BECK:

Question. The actual bill was $50,000 and odd, and the bill as presented to the Legislature and passed was $95,000?

Answer. Yes, sir.

Question. Was there not an investigating committee appointed by the House of Representatives to look into alleged election frauds in the case of Reid and somebody?

Answer. Yes, sir.

Question. Reid and who?

Answer. Reid and Hoge.

Question. Of which Joe Crews was chairman?

Answer. Yes, sir.

Question. What was the amount spent in that investigation?

Answer. The bill brought in there for expenditures was an enormous bill; I do not remember the amount exactly.

Question. Do you remember about the amount? Was it not $68,000?

Answer. It seems to me it was between $60,000 and $70,000.

Question. I want to call your attention to the Dunbar fee.

Answer. At any rate, this was in the bill: $7,500 was charged in the bill by Crews, who made out the expenses, for lawyers' fees and services.

Question. Paid to whom?

Answer. To James Dunbar, of the firm of Chamberlain, Dunbar, and somebody else. Of course it was talked of, and Dunbar very promptly came forward and said that he had never received a dollar, that he had never rendered any services, had never been consulted, and had never received a dollar. The other members of the committee say they never consulted any lawyers at all, because Wright, one of the associate justices of the State now, and Elliott, were both on the committee. They say they discussed the propriety of calling in legal advice, but, as both of them were lawyers, they did not call in any at all. This bill was a gross fabrication; they never consulted any lawyer at all, and Dunbar says they never paid him a dollar. The Attorney-General was instructed to take steps to indict Crews for embezzling the public money. Crews went before the committee investigating this matter, and told them at the very offstart that he did not intend to answer any question that would criminate himself. As soon as they commenced questioning him about this money, and if he paid it to Dunbar, he said, "I decline to answer that question," and so on throughout. And when he was threatened afterward with being indicted, he defied them and said that they did not dare to do it; that they would first have to make an appropriation to enlarge the penitentiary, for he would put the half of them in there.

By Mr. VAN TRUMP:

Question. What did he mean—half of the Legislature?

Answer. The whole concern connected with the government, I suppose.

By Mr. Beok :

Question. And the prosecution was dropped ?

Answer. Yes, sir ; and the money has been drawn and paid.

By Mr. Stevenson :

Question. What money do you mean ?

Answer. The bill he reported for expenses has been paid.

Question. Paid before or after the investigation ?

Answer. Paid before the investigation. The money was done paid and gone ; he rendered in his account and drew the money, and it was too late to get it back.

By the Chairman :

Question. Did he file any receipt for that money ?

Answer. No, sir ; he could not produce any receipt at all.

Question. Did he get the money without a receipt ? How did he get the money ?

Answer. I do not know ; they have so many ways of doing this thing that I cannot tell about this.

By Mr. Beok :

Question. Crews reported this $68,000, or whatever it was, as expenses, and the House ordered it to be paid ?

Answer. Yes, sir.

Mr. Van Trump's report adds this item to the transaction :

The excess of disbursement in the item for fitting up portions of the State-House will be better understood when we state the fact, as proved by the testimony, that, under the pretense of fitting up committee-rooms, the private lodging-rooms at the private boarding-houses of the members, in many instances, were furnished with Wilton and Brussels carpets, mirrors, sofas, etc.

CHAPTER XXV.

On General Legislative Corruption.

THE committee who have examined and the witnesses who have testified in regard to the corruption and fraud in South Carolina legislation, all agree in their testimony. Nobody undertakes to deny its existence, and there is little or no difference of opinion as to its degree. It is complete and universal. It overspreads the State like an inundation.

We extract first from the report of Judge Poland, of the joint congressional committee:

The general venality of the Legislature is complained of, in connection with fraudulent bills for furnishing the State-House, with the passage of bills for aid to railroads, for charters of incorporation, and, indeed, the charge is so general as almost to prevent specification. Like all such indiscriminate charges, it is doubtless exaggerated; but that there was too much foundation for it in truth, the whole tenor of the testimony leaves no room to doubt.

The political party in power must, of course, bear the responsibility of its partisan administration, but the individual dishonesty of the members of either party in public trust, or of private citizens who bribe them, should be treated not as a party fault, so as to give it even the slightest party support, but as a gross departure from duty, meriting the scorn of all honest men, and teaching the man guilty of it that he forfeits the respect of all parties; that no party distinction or services can atone for the lack of personal integrity.

Judge Carpenter, on this subject, says:

Besides this increase of the indebtedness of the State, the general conduct of the Legislature was very unsatisfactory to the people. It was very well understood at Columbia, and throughout South Carolina, that no bill, having any other purpose than a mere public law, could be passed in that Legislature without bribery. The Governor, in his testimony before the joint committee on the Blue Ridge Railroad, has expressed it very strongly. I do not pretend to indorse that statement precisely, but my belief is that of every other man in South Carolina, of any intelligence, that no act was passed there, other than of a purely legal character, that the Legislature was not bribed to pass. I make that statement not only from general information, but from the confessions of a large number of parties interested, the lobby members and the members of the Legislature themselves, who never made any secret of it.

By Mr. BECK to Mr. SUBER:

Question. How have they managed their railroad transactions; do you know any thing about that?

Answer. The Legislature has been charged with corruption in railroad jobs, too. The railroad on which I live, the Greenville & Columbia Railroad, was purchased more than a year ago by a ring, as it is called, in Columbia, headed by the Governor of the State, and with Parker, the Treasurer of the State, and others of that party in it. The stock of that road was purchased at a very low figure;

the stock belonging to the stock-holders along the line of the road was sold out at a very small figure, and it now belongs to the ring, and at the last session of the Legislature a bill was introduced to give the State indorsement to $2,000,000 of the bonds of that road.

Question. After those men had obtained it?

Answer. Yes, sir; after those men obtained it; the bill was introduced the past year, but it was defeated in the Senate. It was believed that they managed to get it through the House by bribery.

Question. What was the general impression about bribes being paid to members of the Legislature for all sorts of jobs; did you ever hear them say any thing on that subject themselves?

Answer. A colored member from my county told me on the floor of the House, the second time I was ever in the House, that he constantly saw bribes offered there to parties to vote for measures; that they had been offered to him. He approached me as I entered the bar of the House, and asked my opinion about some bill that was pending—what I thought of it. The bill, I think, was called the sterling loan bill. He said they were agitating it then, and he was doubtful which way to vote; that he had voted against it the night before, for the reason that he saw men offering bribes to members of the Legislature to vote for it, and he therefore thought that there was something wrong about it; that bribes were constantly being offered in the House for various measures. I have heard that stated generally; but he is the only member of the Legislature who ever told me so.

Question. The members of the Legislature were generally believed to be corrupt, were they not?

Answer. Yes, sir.

Mr. Aldrich, of Barnwell, said:

Question. Do you know of any case of corruption committed by your county officers?

Answer. Well, sir, their administration of the affairs of the county is very bad, very lamentable. They collected $40,000 or $50,000 from the people, yet the roads are not repaired, the bridges are not built, the public buildings are not sufficient for the accommodation of the people, and the claims of the county have not been paid.

Question. Is it the general opinion of the people of your county that the taxes are collected?

Answer. Yes, sir; all the taxes are collected, but the money is squandered.

Question. Is the same thing true in regard to State officers?

Answer. Yes, sir, generally charged so; and I know of some instances of my own knowledge which show that they are more or less corrupt.

Question. Is that the opinion of the white people generally in reference to the State government?

Answer. Yes, sir.

Question. Is it the universal opinion?

Answer. Yes, sir; I think it is, so far as I have been through the State. I have canvassed the State twice, and I have heard that charge made by every man I met.

The Hon. J. E. Stevenson observes:

It is generally admitted that the Legislature has been extravagant, and has made unnecessary, and, in some cases, corrupt appropriations, some of which have been vetoed by the Governor, and defeated, and others passed over his veto. And where extraordinary expenses were necessary for the safety of the State, as to supply arms and ammunition to suppress violence, advantage has been taken by individuals to secure exorbitant gains.

Even the recent investigation by a joint committee of the Legislature to detect corruption is followed by charges, sustained by proofs, that members of the committee, and men connected with it, were more anxious to make illegitimate profits to themselves than to perform their duty. It is charged, and in evidence, that there has been corruption in the Legislature in connection with acts conferring or extending corporate privileges, and that bribery has prevailed.

The following is from the proceedings of the Tax-payers' Convention held in 1871.

The members of that convention thus spoke of the corruption of the government officials:

Indeed, the members of the Senate and the House of Representatives, as well as the officials, do not hesitate openly to charge each other with fraud and corruption; and there is a well-settled tariff for legislative action of this kind most accurately graduated.

A considerable portion of the last session of the Legislature was consumed in mutual criminations of this kind, and one of the Senators actually proclaimed his independence of investigations of fraud and corruption, on the ground that his own frauds would bear investigation quite as well as those of his accusers, and the challenge was not accepted. The Governor of the State, in his veto of a bill for legislative expenses the last session, says: "I regard the money already appropriated during this session, and the sum included in this bill, amounting in the aggregate to $400,000, as simply enormous for one session. It is beyond the comprehension of any one, how the General Assembly could legitimately expend one-half that amount of money." And the matter turned out to be a fraud, as the Governor insinuates. Last winter a committee of both branches of the Legislature was appointed to investigate the frauds and blackmailing connected with the Blue Ridge Railroad legislation of the previous session. The Governor, the main witness, appeared before this committee, and accused the former Legislature of all sorts of villainy. Alluding to the bill granting aid to the road, the Governor says: "When the bill came up a member of the House came to one of the parties and said, 'The report can't go through until I get $500.'" And when an injunction was served on the fiscal officers of the State to prevent the indorsement of the bonds, the Governor alleges that the parties procuring the injunction proposed to withdraw the same if $25,000 would be paid. After many clear and explicit charges of fraud and corruption, the Governor, with an honest burst of indignation against this corrupt body, says: "I know of the fact, or have been told so by a hundred different persons, that money had been paid to get a report through at the last session. . . . I learned afterward that they privately demanded of the president of the road $500 apiece, as it was publicly stated by themselves that they did not get enough out of the road when the bill passed."

CHAPTER XXVI.

The New-York Financial Agency.

ONE of the things from which South Carolina has most suffered, and is now suffering, is the character of its New-York financial connections. Its agent is a man unknown to fame, who has been intrusted with large sums in the bonds of the State, and of whom everybody concerned complains that no satisfactory accounts of his operations in the State securities can be obtained. A good deal more than this is charged, and still more suspected, as will be found by what follows.

It should also be added that it is alleged that his influence was active at the last session of the Legislature in preventing the execution of the desire to verify the actual amount of State bonds on the market, by procuring a registration by the holders. Judge Carpenter's examination on this question elicited the following response:

Question. I want you now to tell this committee how much money was deposited with Kimpton, the financial agent of the State; for what purpose; how it was drawn; upon whose orders; what contract was made with him about it; and who he is.

Answer. After Governor Scott was elected, the Repub-

lican party concluded that they must have a financial
agent in New York, and this man, H. H. Kimpton—whom
nobody, it appears, knows, either in New York or anywhere else, as a financial man—was appointed that agent.
He is a young man with no reputation, I hear. Bonds of
the State were put in his hands to the amount of $2,700,-
000. He gave no security, and no contract has ever been
made with him at all. As the State authorities wanted
money for their various purposes, they drew on him and
he advanced the money.

Question. Either by the sale or the hypothecation of
the bonds of the State ?

Answer. Altogether by the hypothecation of the bonds,
I think. We paid about 15½ per cent. interest for the
money, according to his account, and his commission is to
be added to that. It appears there has never been any
settlement with him at all. I looked over his report; he
reports in a line and a half to the Controller-General, simply saying, "Herewith is my statement," and then he gives
simply the amount received in bonds and the amount drawn
in cash. He says nothing about interest, commission, or
any thing else.

The minority of the joint congressional committee express themselves thus. Speaking of the
Legislative examination, they say :

The committee afterward turned their attention to the
financial agency established in New York, through which
a large amount of the business of the State was transacted,
and they show that there, as in the books of the officials in
South Carolina, the truth was concealed whenever it suited
the purposes of the officials to conceal it. On pages 245
and 246 of their report, they say :

The committee are compelled to say that the financial

agent has acknowledged to them " the incorrectness of his accounts, and admitted that he was directed by the financial board not to make real but fictitious entries; so frightfully large were the expenses of the transactions of the agency, in negotiations of loans, etc., the board thought it best to keep the true amounts in disguise."

Besides this admission of the agent, the manner in which his books and accounts have been kept justifies suspicion as to their accuracy.

The committee most unhesitatingly and emphatically assert that no business man, with honest intentions, who makes his books the true record of his operations, would suffer such an incomplete and questionable account to be kept as the financial agent of South Carolina has kept.

What, however, is our astonishment and indignation when we are told, on finding specified charges, that " they are not correct," that " even detail in payments is no assurance of accuracy ? " And what our humiliation when we are told " the financial board of the State have recommended the covering up and withholding of the real business transactions of the agency ? " — that, because the credit of the State is so low, the standing of the agency so poor, the demands per cent. so great, and the charges for outside financial operations so enormous, to negotiate loans in behalf of the State it would be unwise to be honest, impolitic to tell the truth, unfinancial to let the books become a faithful record !

The same legislative committee continue :

The accounts, books, and vouchers of the financial agent, for the fiscal year ending October, 1871, have not been examined, as has been already stated, nor was there time so to do, and perfect the report which is now presented ; nor were the committee allowed to see them.

While this declaration may be denied by the agent, it is sufficient to say that, while no direct refusal of books, etc., was made, his continued and purposed delays—his own absence from his office under false assurances of sickness, and the fidelity of the confidential clerk to his master, exhibited in his frequent declaration, "I cannot let you see the books, or accounts, or vouchers, unless Mr. Kimpton gives me the order so to do"—all these multiplied pretenses and designs were equal, in their results, to a forbidden examination, and prevented investigation.

Although we are now told that his books and papers are open to the inspection of those who doubt or who are inclined to verify ".the last statement of the management and condition of the finances of the State," yet, from the knowledge the committee has gained, they do not hesitate to say that such an advertisement is like the spider's parlor invitation to the fly, and whoever accepts the invitation will find himself " caught at last," with promises never to be fulfilled, by one who is an adept at trickery, if nothing more.

The committee desire to impress upon the General Assembly the necessity, by further legislation, of clothing them with an immediate authority, unquestioned in detail and prerogative, to examine the books and papers of the financial agent for the fiscal year ending October, 1871, that they may be enabled to complete their supplemental report, which is in an advanced state of preparation, and necessary to perfect the work assigned them, viz., "a complete and thorough examination of all the accounts of the State Treasurer, Controller-General, and financial agent, since their induction into office."

At the Tax-payers' Convention in 1871, while the bonds of the State had not yet fallen to less than 70 to 80 cents on the dollar, a committee of that body reported as follows on Mr. Kimpton's accounts :

The arrangement of having a financial agent in New York does not make a favorable impression upon the committee. Copies of the accounts rendered by him for the fiscal years of 1869 and 1870 are annexed to this report for reference, marked respectively B and C.

The large sum in money or bonds always in the hands of the agent is attended with unusual risk in the management of the finances of a State ; and the difficulty of keeping the accounts of the agency of the Treasury in constant and regular accord is great. It will be seen, for example, by account "B," that, at the end of the year, the total of the sums charged to the Treasurer by Mr. Kimpton was $1,007,924.54, while the sums credited to Mr. Kimpton by the Treasurer amounted to only $623,000 ; exhibiting a discrepancy of $384,924.54, or disagreement of $384,924.-54. In like manner, account "C" exhibits a disagreement of $294,726.92.

It is true these accounts were recently brought into reconcilement, or rather into conformity, with the accounts of the agency. There is added to both an account of the subsequent interest by which this was effected. It will be seen that among the items brought to the credit of the account by the subsequent entries, are these, viz. :

Account (B) fiscal year 1869, for expenses, including
    interest as explained to the committee.......... $64,996 71
Account (C) fiscal year 1870, for expenses, includ-
    ing interest....................................   94,977 42
                                             —————
        Total.................................... $159,974 13

These appear to have been passed to the credit of the agency without being audited. The committee understood Mr. Parker, the Treasurer, to say that he had not received an account of the several items of expense that go to make up the two sums of $64,996.71, and of $94,977.42. These charges, as will hereafter be shown, add enormously to the interest of the public debt, nor is this the end. The committee learned from Mr. Kimpton, that his own proper commission as agent was not included in the above sums. These appear to have been the quarterly balances due to Mr. Kimpton, by the Treasury:

October 1, 1869	$515,424	54
January 1, 1870	180,009	54
April 1, 1870	548,347	84
July 1, 1870	573,317	21
October, 1, 1870	880,843	95
Total	$2,697,943	08

This sum, divided by the five periods, gives an average of $539,588.61, as the sum of the advances, and seven and a half months as the period of time for which they were made. The interest and other charges, as shown in another part of this report, was for twelve months $94,-777.42, or $7,914.78 per month. For seven and a half months it is $59,360.85, or at the rate of 17 per cent. per annum. And to this is yet to be added the agent's commissions. Mr. Kimpton is under the impression that his average advance was greater than the sum stated by your committee. But even if it was $700,000 instead of $539,-588.61, the interest (without his commission) would amount still to the high rate of 13¼ per cent. per annum.

The loss sustained by the State in this mode of dealing is obvious, and it is augmented apparently by the fact that all this risk, expense, and trouble, resulted in the sale of only $1,000,000 of bonds, and these at the moderate rate of 70 per centum. The act providing for the payment of the interest on the public debt in gold had been passed, and had added very largely to the annual charge.

10

State of South Carolina, in Account with

Dr.

Date	Description	Amount	
1871. October 1..	To Balance, as per account received...	$1,267,075	63
	Interest account transferred	259,520	02
	Land Com. account transferred, per drafts omitted in previous account.................	1,500	00
		$1,528,095	65
Dec. 31....	To Balance	$1,528,095	65
	Gold and coupon account transferred..................	15,345	35
1872. January 2..	State Investigating Com. account..	5,700	60
March 31..	Bal. Sinking Fund account transferred as per account rendered..	94,315	26
		$1,643,456	86
1872. March 31..	To Balance	$1,643,456	86
June.....	State Treasurer..................	100,000	00
1872. June 30....	To Balance	$1,743,456	86
Sept. 30...	Interest and Commission account transferred	123,416	66
	Expense account transferred......	885	75
		$1,867,759	27
1872. Sept. 30...	To Balance	$629,415	26

H. H. Kimpton, Financial Agent.

Cr.

1871. Dec. 31....	By Balance.........................	$1,528,095 65
1872. March 31..	By Balance.........................	$1,643,456 86
1872. June 30....	By Balance.........................	$1,643,456 86
1872. Sept. 30...	By transfer account sales 4,214¼ S. C. Bonds....................... Balance .... On hand, $1,656,500 S. C. Bonds, which is including $200,000 S. C. Bonds account Sinking Fund account ; also $598,000 Blue Ridge R. R. Bonds.............	$1,238,344 01 629,415 26 $1,867,759 27

Hon. J. L. NEAGLE, *Controller-General :*

DEAR SIR: The above is my report to date, September 30, 1872.

(Signed)   H. H. KIMPTON,

Financial Agent State S. C.

By R.

The preceding statement of Mr. Kimpton is the last of his favors that have seen the light. It appears in the last annual report of the Controller (1873). It is remarkable in two particulars: It shows a recent sale of $4,214,500 of South Carolina bonds for the sum of $1,238,344 ; and it exhibits charges of $382,936 for interests and commissions on a balance of $1,267,000—all in the accounts of a single year.

CHAPTER XXVII.

On Some Causes of Violence and Disorder.

The following testimony of Judge Carpenter is of such an instructive character in regard to several points that have come under review, and in respect to others not treated, that we make room for it:

Question. What effect did that pardoning of criminals have upon the lawlessness that existed, the taking of the law by men wrongfully in their own hands?

Answer. I think that that, and the manner in which the election was conducted, the election law, and the other matters I have stated—I think these are the sole causes for men taking the law into their own hands. There was a great deal of excitement, a great sense of insecurity, and a great feeling of indignation. Because, in addition to what I have stated, in all the appointments in every department of the government, the men were generally not only corrupt but utterly incompetent. Men were appointed school commissioners who could neither read nor write, at a salary of a thousand dollars a year for a commissioner in each county. Salaries were increased everywhere. Public officers were multiplied, and the only business of the officers seemed to be to prey upon the people. The whole government in all its ramifications seemed to be intent upon no other purpose than self-aggrandizement at the expense of the population, and I confess that I shared in the belief that there was no protection of person or property in the State.

Question. And that even the conviction of criminals did not tend to produce punishment?

Answer. In the first place, the juries, being composed of colored people, as well as of white (parts of each), it was difficult to indict anybody. The moment a question of indictment came, there would be some difficulty of race about it. I think there was none with the white people; but, of course, the colored people had a strong predilection for their own race, and they were not very clear in their ideas of the difference between right and wrong. Then, if the parties were indicted, it was very difficult to convict them; and, if they were convicted, they were very sure to be pardoned. I have known, in more than one instance, where a man preferred a charge against a party, the accused was discharged by the grand-jury, and the accuser indicted for false imprisonment, or something of that sort. In Christ Church Parish, four indictments were found, that my successor on the bench said were an outrage, and he was a simon-pure Scott man. Some colored men had been stealing some cattle, and the owner had them arrested and taken before a justice of the peace, and they were bound over for trial, the proof being very clear. The jury were nearly all colored men, and were summoned by the sheriff of my county—a man of very extreme partisan views—Mr. Mackey, son of Dr. Mackey. The jury discharged the prisoners for stealing the cattle, and indicted the two young planters for false imprisonment. The case was tried at the last June session, at Charleston, by my successor. I have information that it was not a singular case. It has been repeatedly done there. In that case, the judge charged the jury that there was no ground at all.

Question. Would not a course of conduct of that sort deter men from seeking the law as a means of protection?

Answer. Undoubtedly it would.

Question. You say that was not confined to one locality?

Answer. It occurred several times in my circuit, and I had information that it occurred in other circuits. I do not want to be understood as justifying the proceedings of these secret organizations. I do not think it was a remedy for any thing; but in my opinion it was the condition of things which I have detailed that was the cause of it. In my judgment, nothing could be further from a cause for this organization than any hostility to the Federal Government in any of its departments. It had nothing more to do with the Federal Government than it had to do with the Government of China. Whatever may have been their reasons—whether well founded or ill founded—they acted upon the idea that they were without a government to protect them; on the contrary, that the Government was inimical to the white people of the State particularly, protecting their enemies—the men who committed crimes against them—and rewarded them rather than punished them. In my judgment, that was the reason for forming that organization in South Carolina. As I have said before, I do not approve of it, for I think it was a remedy for nothing.

Question. In what way did they obtain and maintain that sort of control?

Answer. They obtained the control originally by the white people of South Carolina refusing to take any part in the elections in the organization of the State. These men then went to the colored people, and said: " We are your friends; we are going into this thing, and have you educate your children, and make every thing better for you," and all that sort of thing. They got their confidence and control. The white people did not go among them. The colored people in that way were made inimical to the white people, and led to think that their interests were antagonistic to the interests of the white people. The white people held the property and what little money there was. The colored people were taught by these men to believe that the lands properly belonged to them and not to their former masters; that the dwelling-houses and gin-houses, and every thing else, belonged to them. I heard that repeatedly stated on the stump last summer, not only by colored men, but by white men. Senator Beverly Nash, a colored man, at Columbia, a very shrewd, sharp, keen man, in a public speech to six or eight thousand men, said to them: "The reformers complain of taxes being too high. I tell you they are not high enough. I want them taxed until they put these lands back where they belong, into the hands of those who worked for them. You toiled for them, you labored for them, and were sold to pay for them, and you ought to have them." That was the key-note of the whole stumping from the sea-coast to the mountains. Some of the people did not say any thing about it; but it was a fierce contest from beginning to end, to array race against race. Our efforts were directed to harmonize the two races for political purposes and legal purposes.

Question. In your canvass, you and the men associated with you had in view the harmonizing of the races?

Answer. Yes, sir.

Question. Did not your safety consist in that course being pursued?

Answer. I think the safety of the whole State and of the people of the State consisted in it. If, after the election was over, these appeals had been kept up to the colored people, and they had acted upon these suggestions, of course there could have been nothing but war. A great many gin-houses and dwelling-houses have been burned by the colored men during the last two or three years in South Carolina.

Question. Do you think that was done at the instigation of others?

Answer. Well, I do not say that, because I do not know it.

Question. Why were they burned, do you think?

Answer. I think it was oftener the result of personal ill-will toward the owners than a preconcerted political design. I am not prepared to think there was any concerted design about it. Of course, an uncultivated wild man, like the uncultivated colored man of South Carolina, subject to very strong passions and impressions, if he thinks he has been particularly ill-treated or any thing of that sort, is very likely to take a fearful revenge. While they are a very gentle people, when they do commit crime they are more barbarous than any people I have seen. In several cases of murder that came before me, sometimes the man would have twenty bullet-wounds. In one case in particular, not only was his head cut off, but he had four or five stabs in the right breast; his heart was literally pierced four or five times, stabbed through and through, and then he was disemboweled. They are a very peaceable people naturally, and, if let alone, they want to do right; but when their passions overcome them, and they commit crime, they do it with a vengeance.

Question. Their ignorance, their peculiar disposition, and their liability to be misled, are well known to the white people of South Carolina?

Answer. Yes, sir. Still there is a great deal of kind feeling toward them on the part of the white people, and a

great deal of kind feeling toward the whites from a large
class of the colored people. The colored men who are not
either local or State politicians, who have any intelligence,
generally feel very kind to the whites, and come to them
if they want any help about any thing—if they want to
borrow any money or get any help of that sort. A great
many of them have very excellent credit, and are of good
character.

Question. What I am coming to is this: with these
known characteristics of the negro, their ignorance and
liability to be imposed upon, and the opinion generally
prevailing throughout the State of the way in which they
have been induced to have hard feelings toward the
whites, will you state to the committee what effect it had
upon the people and their sense of security when the Governor armed them as State militia, and refused to arm the
white people in the same way?

Answer. Well, sir, the people felt they had no security
at all; that they might be attacked at any time. I do not
think myself that this militia was ever organized for the
purpose of any war on the white people. It was organized
to carry the election through the colored vote; to intimi-
date and overawe the colored people. I do not think they
ever intended to have any fight with the white people,
but, of course, the white people felt very anxious upon the
subject, hearing companies of colored men drilling and
training every night in each village of two or three thousand inhabitants, and the people were perfectly unpro-
tected. In the time of election there was a great deal of
whisky about, for the colored man is not very much unlike
his white brother in that respect; he is very fond of whisky.
And it is very astonishing to me the paucity of casualties
and crimes that occurred in consequence of it. They
seemed to content themselves with carrying out the ideas

of the party.   On the day of election they were parading, and then, not where there were many white people, but in the dense colored districts, they overawed and drove off everybody that was obnoxious to them.   I think that was the original purpose of the militia, for certainly Governor Scott was in the army too long to suppose that this militia would be effective in any contest with the white people of South Carolina.   I think he has expressed himself very fully on that subject; he knows that they are of no consequence for that purpose.

Question. Was there any thing in the militia law that prevented the organization of white men as militia, and their being armed as such ?

Answer. No, sir.   Under the law the Governor had the right to receive any organization for militia purposes; the Governor had to receive them.   Any who chose could propose to form a company, but they had to ask the Governor to receive them.   If he received them, very well; they could go on organizing; but it was made a very serious offense to drill and organize a company without the permission of the Governor.   When a white company was organized and offered to the Governor he invariably refused it, until very lately.   I believe he received a white company from Columbia, and perhaps one from some other place. It was made a highly-penal offense to organize a company without the permission of the Governor.   All other military organizations were prohibited, except those he accepted, and he accepted nothing but colored militia.

Question. They were generally composed of his own political friends?

Answer. Entirely so.

CHAPTER XXVIII.

On the Supply of Arms and Ammunition for the Alleged Defense of the State.—The Governor's Pardons.

GOVERNOR SCOTT, being concerned about his reëlection in 1870, set on foot various contrivances to make it secure.

They are described in the following extracts. The substance of the State investigation committee's report, composed of men of Governor Scott's own party, is, that he spent $374,000 of the public money to get himself rechosen. His Republican adversary in the canvass, Hon. R. B. Carpenter, adds that he emptied the prisons with the same object, and filled all his offices with corrupt mercenaries, and otherwise showed himself a master in the art of South Carolina politics.

The committee, composed of Republicans, on page 10, speaking of the cost and management of "Scott's militia," say :

This part of the work of the present administration, so severely and extendedly criticised at home and abroad, so fruitful of suspicion and opposition among a large portion of our citizens, as well as dissatisfaction to another class, while intended for the preservation of the peace, lives, and property of the people of the State, has not only failed in its avowed object, and been managed unwisely, but also proved an expensive experiment, as the charges for such purpose will show the total outlay for the enrollment and organization of the militia, now entirely without organization, the armed force now virtually disarmed, the purchase of arms, one thousand Winchester rifles, now scattered throughout the thirty-one counties of the State, the sum of $171,009.93.

The committee are, in this connection, forced to the acknowledgment, however unpleasant or humiliating it may be to such as are connected with the fact, that the moneys expended (as vouchers indicated the direction in which the funds were used) were not all paid out for such purposes. In the enrollment and organization of the militia, as well as in the armed force employed by the Governor, there was a most ample and complete opportunity for ambitious political partisans and aspirants for reëlection to arm and equip a force of personal friends and advocates, and pay them "when on service the same pay and allowances as are given to officers and soldiers of the same grade in the Army of the United States," not out of their own purse, but "out of any moneys in the Treasury not otherwise appropriated; the State to be reimbursed by a special tax upon any county into which the Governor was compelled to send an armed force." And to carry out these provisions, the Governor was to exercise all the powers conferred upon him by an act entitled "An act to suppress insurrection and rebellion," passed September 22, 1868. Besides, as he was to be the judge of the existence, in any county, of the necessity of an armed force "to preserve the peace," and it was his own prerogative to commission the officers and subalterns, and indorse their pay accounts.

An enrolled, organized, and armed retinue of personal favorites or advocates were commissioned and placed upon his staff at the proper time, as well as ordered to form companies, battalions, regiments, and brigades, throughout the State, into what was called "The National Guard," *alias* "Scott's militia." This statement is made from undoubted evidence in the premises, and cannot be controverted. The election in 1870 was carried, in part, by the means herein stated, and while some portion of the funds appropriated for the purposes specified were, no doubt, expended for the same, the largest amounts were diverted to secure the reëlection of Robert K. Scott, as Governor of South Carolina, but not for the success of the Republican party. That the Adjutant-General has not known of this diversion of special appropriations, cannot be possible; for, being a member of the House of Representatives, the Speaker of the House, and signer of all bills passed both branches of the General Assembly, he must be familiar with the laws passed; and, as the elected Adjutant-General, the principal staff-officer of the State, whose recognized duty is to assist the commander-in-chief in the details of military organization, and promulgate his orders, he certainly cannot claim entire ignorance in the use of the funds which are here referred to.

Nor is this all. A more glaring robbery of the Treasury, for personal ambition and gain, has been perpetrated, and will be presented in that part of this report which covers the investigation of the financial agent's books and papers. The enormous sum of $202,602.66 (two hundred and two thousand six hundred and two dollars and sixty-six cents) not appearing anywhere upon the State Treasurer's books, and never intended for the public eye or ear, has been paid, in addition to the amount already aggregated, for the alteration of arms, which swells the account to $374,696.59.

Hon. R. B. Carpenter defined his political position as follows:

It was very well known to the convention that nominated me that I had voted for General Grant, and I had voted for Lincoln for his second term. It was equally well known that I had been appointed by Chief-Justice Chase register of bankruptcy, and equally well known that I had been elected by the first Legislature of South Carolina as judge; that they nominated me as a Republican, and knew I was one.

He then went on in reply to the interrogatories of the congressional committee, and said:

Another cause of discontent was the lavish pardons that were issued by the Governor. Men of the worst character, men who had committed the worst possible crimes, were pardoned and turned loose without any application from anybody, as far as was known; from no responsible parties, certainly; no application from either the judge or solicitor. They were pardoned and turned loose to prey again upon the community. Another cause of discontent was the character of persons appointed to fill offices under the Executive. The constitution of South Carolina gives the Executive vast patronage, or at least the Legislature have assumed it, whether the constitution gives it or not. All the county auditors, county treasurers, trial justices—as they are called there—justices of the peace, and most of the local officers; are appointed by the Governor. As a rule they are utterly incompetent, and as a rule they are utterly corrupt. Another cause of discontent was the organization and arming of the militia of the State, and the furnishing them with ammunition. The militia were confined to colored people. Numerous applications were made by white companies to be received into the State militia, but they were all rejected. Some twenty thousand colored people in different parts of the State were armed with Winchester and Springfield and other rifles, and near the time of election ammunition was distributed to them, as if upon the eve of battle. They were sometimes very offensive, and did a great deal of mischief. It was very offensive to the white people that these colored people should be armed, and sometimes depredations were committed by them; that was a serious cause of discontent. Another cause was the election law itself, and the manner in which it was executed. I do not remember the number of sections in the statute. It is a long act, and from the beginning to the end no penalty is provided for any violation of its provisions. That act places the whole power of conducting the elections in the hands of the three commissioners for each county, to be appointed by the Governor, without confirmation by the Senate. These commissioners, thus appointed, were required, in the first place, to designate and fix the places of voting. They appointed the managers to receive the votes—to have the ballot-boxes at the polls and receive the votes. The law then required the managers, within three days after the election, to return these ballot-boxes sealed up to the commissioners. The commissioners were allowed by law ten days to count these ballots and to make their returns of the persons elected. They began their career as commissioners by being very generally themselves candidates for office; and they had to decide whether they were elected or their competitors. Before the appointment of the commissioners, however, the Executive Committee of the Reform party requested Governor Scott to appoint one reform commissioner for each county. That he declined to do, and, so far as I am apprised, he appointed commissioners only from his own party and his own friends. These commissioners commenced operations by fixing the voting-places upon the banks of rivers, and upon the sea-coast, where the colored population is very dense; while farther back from the rivers, and along the upper part of the State, the white population predominates, but is very scattered. As a rule, the commissioners fixed the voting-places to accommodate the colored people, and to be as far off and inconvenient for the white people as they could. In certain counties the white people would have to travel forty miles to the nearest precinct to vote. Then it was proposed to the Executive Committee of the Republican party to have a committee of each party remain with the ballot-boxes and see that they were not tampered with. This they declined to do, and, except for the city of Charleston, they kept these ballot-boxes in their private houses, from the time of the election until the time they made their returns. That the ballot-boxes were stuffed after the election is no longer a matter of opinion. In some of the counties it has been a matter of judicial investigation. For instance, in the county of Beaufort there was a trial of the commissioners for that county, charged with stuffing the ballot-boxes after the election. The trial was before his honor Judge Bond, of the Circuit Court of the United States. The jury was composed of an equal number of black men and white men. They found the defendants guilty, and Judge Bond sentenced them to the penitentiary for two years each. In counties where it was utterly impossible there should have been a majority for Governor Scott, in my opinion the ballot-boxes were stuffed, the record falsified, and the will of the people entirely thwarted. I cannot suppose that a law of that sort was made for any other purpose than to keep the party in power, to prolong their power, whether the people voted for them or not. I have already stated that a large number of criminals of the worst description were pardoned by Governor Scott. I think the pardons came much the thickest just before the October elections of last year.

Question. What was the date of your election?

Answer. It was on the 19th of October.

Question. The Governor's official statement of pardons by him reaches to the 1st of October?

Answer. Yes, sir.

Question. From your knowledge and information, what would be your opinion as to the number of pardons issued between that date and the date of the election?

Answer. I could not state. I saw several persons that I had myself sentenced to the penitentiary, who were pardoned just before the election; I met them on the streets; three or four of a very bad description of men—men who had been sentenced to the penitentiary for a series of years. I do not know, but I judged, from seeing three or four that I knew myself, that there must have been a great many all over the State; and that is my information from other people. I think the official statement of pardons from October 1, 1869, to October 1, 1870, gives the number as two hundred and five, out of some four hundred and eighty who were in the penitentiary. How many of them had been convicted during that time, and how many of them were there before, I cannot say. I do not know whether the official record, if I had it, would enable me to say. According to General Stolbrand's report, who is the keeper of the penitentiary, two hundred and five prisoners in the penitentiary were pardoned between October 1, 1869, and October 1, 1870, out of some four hundred and eighty who were confined in the penitentiary during that year. I think the pardons were largely in excess of the convictions; I think there must have been more of them there before Governor Scott exercised the pardoning power with so great liberality.

Question. And you think from the 1st of October to the day of election it continued quite liberally?

Answer. Quite liberally, I should think.

Question. But the number you cannot give?

Answer. I cannot give the number for the State.

Question. What effect did the free exercise of pardon have upon the sense of security of all the people throughout the State?

Answer. The same effect it would have anywhere, that there was very little security for life and property in the country.

Question. What effect did it have upon their reliance upon the courts for the proper redress of grievances?

Answer. It had a very bad effect, as I think such an indiscriminate use of the pardoning power will have everywhere. If men can commit crimes with impunity, of course no one will be afraid to do so, especially in such a population as ours.

The minority of the joint committee of Congress, in reporting on this case, say:

The only authority to be found upon the statute-books of South Carolina for the purchase of arms is in the joint resolutions of February 8 and March 16, 1869. The resolution of February 8th authorizes the Governor to employ an armed force to preserve the peace, to consist of one hundred men or more, if in his opinion needed, "who shall be fully armed and equipped." The resolution of March 16th authorizes him "to purchase two thousand stands of arms," to be paid for "out of any money in the Treasury not otherwise appropriated." It will thus be seen that the Governor's power to purchase arms, in any contingency, is limited to two thousand stands; and that this power is still

further restricted to the amount of funds in the Treasury
not otherwise appropriated by law. And yet, Governor
Scott, in the face of this clearly-limited authority, purchased ten thousand stands of breech-loading and Winchester rifles, and one million of centre-coppered car-
tridges.

On the subject of pardons, we give the following from Judge Poland's report, and Governor
Scott's own explanation :

The pardoning power has been exercised freely by the
Executive, and unless we bear in mind the peculiar state
of society existing in this State, the party divisions so
nearly separating the whites and the blacks, the severity
of punishment visited upon the negroes for trivial offenses,
the temptation which would naturally present itself to give
credence to their wrongs when asking for clemency, the
proportion of pardons to the number of convictions seems
at once to establish that the power has been abused. That
it has been exercised in mistake in many instances, as it
often is in all the States, we cannot doubt, after hearing
of the acts of some of the pardoned convicts. But we are
not prepared to give the sweeping condemnation of this
feature of the administration that some of its other feat-
ures deserve.

The reports for the year 1870 show that, in that year
there were in the penitentiary five hundred and seventy-
five convicts, and two hundred and five pardons were
granted.   The Governor's message thus accounts for a
large number of them :

"Such as are enumerated as pardoned mainly consisted of those whose terms were about to expire, and who
were recommended for their good behavior by the superintendent. By anticipating the expiration of their sen-

tence, the criminal generally avoids the deprivation of his civil rights, many of which would be forfeited by their consummation. The effect of this leniency is stated by the superintendent as being most salutary in promoting good behavior among the convicts, and enabling him, from day to day, to designate large numbers of the convicts for work as laborers, teamsters, and mechanics, without the presence of a guard outside the inclosure of the prison, and not one has betrayed the confidence thus reposed in them."

CHAPTER XXIX.

Cumulative Voting as a Remedy.

WE have heretofore suggested minority representation or cumulative voting as one of the resources of the whites of South Carolina in their present straits. On an examination of the proceedings of the Tax-payers' Convention, held at Columbia in May, 1871, it appears the subject was brought up for consideration in that body, and was favorably received.

We extract from the report of the committee on the subject:

The committee to whom was referred the question of the expediency of the cumulative system of voting, or such system as will protect the rights of minorities, ask leave to make the following report:

The means of protecting the rights of minorities, in representative forms of government, has for a long period engaged the attention of thoughtful minds. In Europe, as well as in this country, this question has been fully discussed, and a satisfactory solution anxiously sought. So defective is the system of mere majority rule—so flagrant are the abuses to which it is liable, that the necessity for

its modification strikes with force every impartial observer.
It is obvious that the needs of good government require
that some effective organism be devised for the protection
of minorities. Your committee deem it unnecessary to
enter upon an analysis of the several schemes of proportional representation that have been suggested. Enough
to say that, in our judgment, the plan of cumulative voting best accomplishes the end in view—best makes representation coextensive with the whole body of electors.
This plan obtains wherever there is more than one officer
to be elected. It gives the elector as many votes as there
are persons to be chosen, and allows him to bestow his
votes upon the whole number, or to cumulate them upon any
number less than the whole. The effect of this system is
to give to each political interest in a community a representation proportionate to its numerical strength. Under its
operation the true office of suffrage, which is to collect the
sense of a whole community, will be subserved. There is
effected neither exclusive representation of the majority,
nor exclusive representation of the minority ; but proportional representation. The proposition is that the cumulative system secures thorough and general representation
of all the interests in the political body.

Your committee are of the opinion that, abstractly
considered, proportional representation is a great govern-
mental principle—a wise, just measure of reform, and one
absolutely necessary to make unlimited suffrage consistent
with peace, order, and security. It enters the political
body as a saving, a conserving element. It comes to leaven
the lump of democracy, and to give the essence of genuine republicanism, which is, briefly stated, thorough and
general representation. But if proportional representation be an admirable system in any government founded
upon the popular will, your committee hold that the plan

is peculiarly applicable to such a condition of society as this State now presents.

Your committee are gratified to state that this system of cumulative voting, which is destined to play so important a part in the development of popular rule, has already been put in operation. "Proposed, explained, and advocated in the first instance by James Garth Marshall, a subject of the crown of Great Britain," this plan has been championed by ex-Senator Buckalew, of this country, has been incorporated in the revised constitution of Illinois, and has been put upon its trial in a Pennsylvania town. Recently the subject has attracted unusual interest in the South. In our own State it has been received with great favor, and lifted above the plane of political partyism.

Governor Scott.

In reply to an inquiry from your committee as to his opinion of minority representation, the Governor was clear and explicit in his indorsement of the plan, believing, as he said, that it would do more to destroy prejudice, prevent ill-feeling, and educate the majority, than any event which could occur.

The Hon. George A. Trenholm, one of the leading Conservatives of the State, sustained the measure.

Mr. Trenholm said:

The principle of universal suffrage as a means of universal representation, commends itself to the approval of right-minded men in all countries. Statesmen oppose themselves to it in vain. It lies at the very foundation of every true republican government, and merits the support of all good citizens. It is not against universal suffrage that we remonstrate; it is against the imperfect application of it. That mode of practical application prevailing, not in South Carolina alone, but in every State in this Union save one; a method by which, instead of universal representation, the entire minority, no matter how large that minority may be, is deprived of all representation whatsoever. It is against this great defect, this monstrous inequality, that we remonstrate, and for which we would institute a remedy. The one recommended by the committee is not new; it has been extensively discussed both in Europe and in this country, and has met with the sanction of many eminent men. In England, that great country, whence we derive many of the most valued lessons of political government; amid an aristocracy of birth, wealth and education, the principle of minority representation has been recognized and incorporated in the Constitution. This was done in 1867; and again in 1870 it was reaffirmed upon a motion to repeal the act of 1867. This motion was opposed by such statesmen as Bright and Gladstone, and defeated. What was the act of 1867, and why did those holding the supremacy in legislative power make the concession it involved? It gave one representative to the minority in every county entitled to three members of Parliament, and it wisely anticipated the time when universal suffrage would unsettle the tenure of political power, when those who now ruled the country might themselves be thrown into the minority.

This principle of minority representation is what is recommended by the committee, and it comes with the sanction of an authority that is of the highest dignity with those on whom the decision of this question devolves. If there is any name revered above all others by the Republicans, it is that of Mr. Lincoln. And what do we perceive in the State from which Mr. Lincoln came? The Legis-

11

lature of Illinois is represented to have been as incompetent as ours—representation as imperfect; and to cure these evils, the same as we are suffering from, they adopted in their election laws the very principle recommended by your committee—the principle of cumulative voting. By a vote of one hundred thousand majority, the people resolved to give to the minority that representation without which universal suffrage is not universal representation.

Having then relinquished much, for which so many of our people suffered and bled and died, may we not call upon our fellow-citizens in the other States to sustain us in this necessary measure of protection? I believe, sir, that they will applaud and support this measure. I do not distrust the people of the North; I have confidence in their sense of justice.

Mr. Chamberlain, the Republican Attorney-General, spoke in the convention, on this subject, as follows:

In the first place, gentlemen, it is necessary to modify the absolute control which a mere numerical majority has obtained over the State, and to secure for intelligence and property a proper representation in the affairs of the government. And, looking about for some device which without violence to the fundamental principle upon which our government rests, will bring relief from the grievances which afflict our people, I have fixed upon this system of cumulative voting, because it is not only just in its theory, but it will prove itself right in its results. It takes nothing from the rights of the majority. It gives them a predominating control, but not an absolute disposition of the entire fortunes of the State. Do you believe for a moment, then, when you put into an ignorant Assembly, many of whom can neither read nor write, forty-seven gentlemen, whom I might select in this body, that you would not shame them into decency, or frighten them from crime? (Applause.) Who does not know that the presence of one honest man puts to flight a band of robbers? Now, according to this system, you deny nothing which belongs to the majority, but, from the moment you place in the Lower House forty-seven of your ablest citizens, bad legislation will cease, and good legislation will begin. Are the opponents of this measure on this floor so intense in their devotion to political ideas that they will refuse a proposition which gives to them a representation of one-third, and a corresponding influence in public affairs? I hope not; for when, by force of political success, they have gathered a majority of the State to their side, there will then be left to us who differ the same rights we are now according to them. Is it not fair, just, right? Its immediate results are relief from present grievances, and it points to the future, where all interests, no matter what may be the political fortunes of the State, will be protected.

Now, I say to you, gentlemen, give us who have to do with making this practicable, something that we can honestly take back to our political associates, and, in the name of the property and intelligence of the State, secure this right. Let there be peace between us now, and prosperity hereafter. Strengthen our hands, who desire to do what in us lies, to make South Carolina safe for every man in his life, career, and private interests. I say, again, it is right. Grant it.

CHAPTER XXX.

Governor Scott on the Legislature.—The Committee of the Legislature on Governor Scott.—Attorney-General Chamberlain on them both.

THERE seems to be no want of evidence of the corruption of South Carolina public officers. We have their unbiassed testimony in relation to one another. In what follows we have what Governor Scott thinks and says of the Legislature, what a committee of that body think and say of him, as well as of other prominent public functionaries, and what the Attorney-General says of both, and of the situation generally.

Speaking of the Governor's political operations in enrolling the militia to promote his own election, the legislative committee of investigation say :

The committee are, in this connection, forced to the acknowledgment, however unpleasant or humiliating it may be to such as are connected with the fact, that the moneys expended (as vouchers indicated the direction in which the funds were used) were not all paid out for such purposes. In the enrollment and organization of the militia, as well as in the armed force employed by the Governor, there was a most ample and complete opportunity for ambitious political partisans and aspirants for reëlection to arm and equip a force of personal friends and advocates, and pay them "when on service the same pay and allowances as are given to officers and soldiers of the same grade in the Army of the United States," not out of their own purse, but "out of any moneys in the Treasury not otherwise appropriated."

Governor Scott on his part utters the following incidental opinion of the Legislature :

STATE OF SOUTH CAROLINA, EXECUTIVE DEPARTMENT, COLUMBIA, *March* 7, 1871.

To the Honorable the Senate of South Carolina :

GENTLEMEN : I return to your honorable body, without my approval, an act appropriating $265,000 for legislative expenses, for the following reasons, to wit :

First, I regard the expenditure of the money already appropriated during this session, and the sum included in this bill, amounting in the aggregate to $400,000, as simply enormous for one session of the Legislature. It is beyond the comprehension of any one how the General Assembly could legitimately expend one-half that amount of money. I cannot refrain from expressing the opinion that there must have been some secret agency in fixing the sum at that amount, as a number of the members, both of the House and Senate, have expressed their surprise at finding the appropriation changed from $125,000, as it was believed to have passed, to that of $265,000. I regret the necessity of returning the act without my approval, on the last day of the session, but to do otherwise I feel would be recreant to the duties imposed upon me, by becoming a party to a wrong by which the whole people would be made to suffer.

I might give many other cogent reasons why this bill
should not become a law, but time prevents my doing
other than giving it my unqualified disapproval, believing
that the members of the General Assembly will themselves
correct an error that must have crept into the bill clandes-
tinely in its enrollment.

Very respectfully,

ROBERT K. SCOTT, *Governor.*

LEGISLATIVE COMMITTEE.

On page 962 of the printed South Carolina
testimony will be found a letter from the present
Attorney-General of the State, Hon. D. H Chamberlain, a pronounced Republican and a native
of Massachusetts; who, as he says in his testimony, "carried his sword to the South, and,
when the war was over, remained there." This
letter is dated May 5, 1871, and is addressed to
Colonel W. L. Trenholm, late Secretary of the
Treasury of the Confederacy. This gentleman
says:

I propose to lay aside all partisanship, and simply to
state facts as I conceive them to exist. Let us look at our
State when the reconstruction acts first took effect in 1868.

A social revolution had been accomplished; an entire
reversal of the political relations of most of our people
had ensued. The class which formerly held all the political powers of our State were stripped of all.

The class which had formerly been less than citizens,
with no political power or social position, were made the sole
depositaries of the political powers of the State. I refer
now to the practical results, not to theories. The numeri-

cal relations of the two races here were such that one race, under the new laws, held absolute political control of the State.

The attitude and action of both races, under these new conditions, while not unnatural, was, I must think, unwise and unfortunate. One race stood aloft and haughtily refused to seek the confidence of the race which was just entering on its new powers; while the other race quickly grasped all the political power which the new order of things had placed within their reach.

From the nature of the case, the one race were devoid of political experience, of all or nearly all education, and depended mainly for all these qualities upon those who, for the most part, chanced to have drifted here from other States, or who, in very rare instances, being former residents of the State, now allied themselves with the other race. No man of common prudence, or who was even slightly familiar with the working of social forces, could have then failed to see that the elements which went to compose the now dominant party were not of the kind which produce public virtue and honor, or which could long secure even public order and peace.

I make all just allowance for exceptional cases of individual character, but I say that the result to be expected, from the very nature of the situation in 1868, was that a scramble for office would ensue among the members of the party in power, which, again, from the nature of the case, must result in filling the offices of the State, local and general, with men of no capacity, and little honesty or desire to really serve the public.

The nation had approved the reconstruction measures, not because they seemed to be free of danger, nor because they were blind to the very grave possibilities of future evils, but in the hope that the one race, wearing its new

laurels, and using its new powers with modesty and forbearance, would gradually remove the prejudices and enlist
the sympathies and coöperation of the other race, until a
fair degree of political homogeneity should be reached,
and race lines should cease to mark the limits of political
parties.

Three years have passed, and the result is—what? Incompetency, dishonesty, corruption in all its forms, have
"advanced their miscreated fronts;" have put to flight
the small remnant that opposed them, and now rule the
party which rules the State.

You may imagine the chagrin with which I make this
statement. Truth alone compels it. My eyes see it—all
my senses testify to the startling and sad fact. I can never
be indifferent to any thing which touches the fair fame of
that great national party to which all my deepest convictions attach me, and I repel the libel which the party bearing that name in this State is daily pouring upon us. I am
a Republican by habit, by conviction, by association; but
my republicanism is not, I trust, composed solely of equal
parts of ignorance and rapacity. Such is the plain statement of the present condition of the dominant party of
our State.

Being afterward examined by the joint committee of Congress, he testified as follows:

Question. Give us some account of the abuses of the
State government of South Carolina.

Answer. I think that, in the first place, the misfortune
was that the dominant party was necessarily made up of
such materials as it was. Of course, negro suffrage was
not acceptable to the former ruling population of the State,
and they refused to have any thing to do with it. That
left a very large numerical majority in the hands of the

negroes of the State, and of the few white men who had
gone there at the close of the war, and the very few white
men who had been residents of the State before and had
joined the Republican party. The material for creating
public officers in those elements was necessarily very poor.

A large number of incompetent and dishonest local
officers were elected throughout the State. Their incapacity and dishonesty was displayed very conspicuously.
In many counties their local affairs have been very much
mismanaged; and in the Legislature we have had a great
deal of corruption.

Question. If I understand you, then, the whole State
government of South Carolina, including all its local details, is in a terrible condition in regard to a fair administration of the public affairs of the State?

Answer. That is a little different from the statement I
would make. I would make this statement: that I think
there are very many abuses existing now in the State,
growing out of the incompetency and dishonesty of Republican office-holders.

Question. You have no personal knowledge of corruption on the part of the office-holders of South Carolina,
have you?

Answer. Well, sir, I think I have personal knowledge;
that is, as much personal knowledge as I have of any thing
that I have not seen with my own eyes.

Question. Outside of the city of Columbia?

Answer. Oh, yes, sir.

Question. Have you seen any thing of it outside of the
city of Columbia?

Answer. Yes, sir.

Question. What?

Answer. Do you want that I should mention where and
who?

Question. I do not care to go into an examination as to the names of parties.

Answer. I can illustrate what I mean. In the county of Newberry, at the last term of court just now closed, two trial justices were indicted for malfeasance in office, and also two of the three county commissioners: the other had run away; they were all four convicted and are now in jail. For instance, the county commissioners were convicted of purchasing supplies, and the party who sold the supplies charged two or three prices for them, and the excess was divided with the county commissioners. The trial justices were convicted of extortion and oppression.

Question. That is a strong Republican county?

Answer. Yes, sir.

Question. Were you present at the trial?

Answer. No, sir.

Question. Was it tried before a jury of colored men?

Answer. Of colored and white men.

Question. A mixed jury?

Answer. A mixed jury.

Question. Then there is no difficulty in convicting these criminals?

Answer. I think not.

Question. Then why the necessity for using these extraordinary means of Ku-klux outrages to put them down?

Answer. That is very true; I think there is no need of it.

Question. Do you know any other instance in which there has been conviction or indictment.

Answer. The three county commissioners of Charleston County are under indictment.

Question. You mean the city of Charleston?

Answer. The county of Charleston, which embraces considerable outlying territory.

Question. Do you know of any others?

Answer. In the county of Williamsburgh, I am not sure whether indictments have been found or not. But a day or two before I left I saw the report of the grand-jury, in which they made similar statements in reference to the conduct of the county officers there; but I will not say that bills of indictment were returned; my impression is that they were.

Question. Have not the Governor and the Executive officers under him been charged with corruption?

Answer. Yes, sir.

Question. To any great extent?

Answer. Oh, yes, sir; very gross charges of corruption have been made.

CHAPTER XXXI.

Taxation.

THE pressure of taxation upon South Carolina is readily exhibited when put in contrast with what it was before the war.

The taxable values of the State in 1860 were $490,000,000. Then the average annual State and county tax was $400,000, which included interest on the public debt. Deducting the value of the slaves, then estimated at $174,000,000, and we have left the sum of $316,000,000. But the decline in all values in the State has reduced the value of this $316,000,000 to $184,000,000 in 1870.

The annual State and county tax now averages about $2,000,000, without reckoning irregularities or frauds in expenditure, which go constantly to swell this sum; and without any appropriations for interest on the public debt.

The contrast stands thus:

Valuation before the war.................	$490,000,000
Taxation before the war.................	400,000
Present valuation.......................	184,000,000
Present taxation........................	2,000,000

Showing that, while the valuation of the property of the State is now a little over one-third of what it was then, the annual State and county taxes are five times as great.

To this charge is to be added the municipal taxation of the towns.

The State Tax-payers' Convention, held in 1871, made these comments, among others, on this subject:

The taxable value of the property of the State, in 1860, was $490,000,000, and the taxes only $392,000; now the taxable property has been reduced to $184,000,000, and the taxes increased to $2,000,000; so, you perceive, while your property has been reduced to less than half its former value, your taxes have been increased 500 per cent.!

The first great wrong is the fearful and unnecessary increase of the public debt. An extraordinary increase is admitted on all hands. The people who have to pay these obligations; those, I mean, who own the property and pay the taxes, are entitled to know the amount and character of the public indebtedness; not merely the actual debt, but all contingent liabilities. A painful uncertainty rests over this matter. Let it be probed to the bottom. If the debt has been over-stated, it will be a great relief to the people to know it. When a clear light is let in upon this matter, we shall know where we are, and be the better able to face the situation and its responsibilities.

Next, the applications of the public moneys have been wild, reckless, and profligate. This is without question; and perhaps never in the history of any people has this profligacy presented a bolder or more shameless front. Corruption here does not hide itself in secret places and dark corners; it stalks abroad, it flaunts itself in the light of day, it assumes the part and bearing of virtue, and openly boasts of its achievements. The end of these things, if not rebuked and checked, will be not only utter demoralization, but certain bankruptcy and ruin.

The direct logical result of increased debt and reckless expenditures is excessive taxation. Not only is the annual tax increased manifold, but, by act of the late session of the Legislature, two tax levies are required to be paid within the limits of one year. This is an intolerable burden, and is calculated, even if it be not intended, to bring about a wide-spread confiscation of property. And the worst feature of the matter is the curious and anomalous fact, without parallel in the history of any representative government, that they who lay the taxes do not pay them, and that they who are to pay them have no voice in the laying of them.

TAXATION AND REPRESENTATION.

The Executive Committee, to whom was referred the grievance of taxation without representation in the taxing body, and to suggest a remedy for the existing evil, beg leave to report, that the present political and financial condition of South Carolina is a forcible and melancholy illustration of the evils resulting from taxation without representation. . . . Mr. Lathers said: I cannot refrain from calling your attention to the expenditures of the county commissioners of Charleston for the current year ending October last, amounting to $238,841. The Governor in his messages, transmitting the same to the Legislature, properly remarks that "these amounts are of startling magnitude, and it is worthy of consideration whether they cannot be materially reduced." I believe an investigation connected with these frauds has been had or proposed.

ITEMS.

Roads and bridges............................	$108,225
Public buildings...............................	28,679
Constables and trial justices...................	38,866
Sheriff, clerk of county, and coroner...........	62,671
Total.....................................	$238,841

Perhaps before the war these items would have reached $50,000 to $75,000. Trial justices, State constables, and herds of expensive and useless officials, are rapidly corrupting the people and eating out their substance.

When we reflect that this is the expense of but one of the thirty-odd counties of the State, spending over a quarter of a million under the power of a mere commission, we need not be surprised that the taxes of the State this year reach over $2,000,000, against less than $400,000 before the war. As the tax to be paid this year aggregates over $4,000,000, as it includes two levies which is tenfold the amount paid before the war in any one year, we may well be constrained to look to our rulers for some mitigation, and ask for a convention of tax-payers to consider the grave issues which the ignorance and fraud of the Legislature are precipitating upon us in a practical confiscation of our property by taxation.

The following is from the minority report of the joint committee of Congress :

Salaries in South Carolina for the Fiscal Year ending September 30, 1855, as per Report of the Controller-General for 1855.

Governor.................................	$3,500 00
Governor's private secretary..............	500 00
Governor's messenger.....................	250 00
Chancellors and judges...................	30,000 00

Brought forward..........................	$34,250	00
Attorney-General and solicitors...............	5,600	00
Clerks, etc., Court of Appeals...............	1,700	00
Libraries of Court of Appeals...............	400	00
State Reporter.............................	1,500	00
Controller-General.........................	2,000	00
Two Treasurers.............................	3,600	00
Commissioner of Public Works.............	150	00
Adjutant and Inspector General.............	2,500	00
Quartermaster-General	500	00
Arsenal-keepers and physician.............	1,900	00
Secretary of State.........................	800	00
Port physician.............................	800	00
Controller's clerk.........................	750	00
Assessor of St. Philip's and St. Michael's...	800	00
President and seven professors South Carolina College........................	20,500	00
Officers South Carolina College.............	1,700	00
Total.............................	$79,450	00
Salaries year ending October 31, 1870......	$205,439	18
Salaries year ending September 30, 1855....	79,450	00
Difference.........................	$125,989	18

Gross Amount of Taxes assessed and collected in South Carolina for Five Years prior to the War, to wit, from 1851 to 1855, inclusive.

Gross taxes, under act of 1850, for year 1851...............................	$515,678	88
Gross taxes, under act of 1851, for year 1852...............................	349,931	28
Gross taxes, under act of 1852, for year 1853...............................	361,775	87

Brought forward......................	$1,227,386 03
Gross taxes, under act of 1853, for year 1854............................	429,975 99
Gross taxes, under act of 1854, for year 1855............................	399,739 67
Total for five years...............	$2,057,101 69

This was a levy upon a property basis of $490,000,000, including slaves at a low valuation. The special tax upon slaves for the year 1855 was the sum of $231,117.60—in the year 1870, upon a property basis, at a high valuation, excluding, of course, the value of the emancipated slave population of $174,000,000, there was levied and collected the sum of $2,265,047, or $107,945.31 more than the aggregate taxation, on more than double the amount of property, for five consecutive years prior to the war.

The assessment of the real property of the State, made prior to the sitting of that convention, showed a valuation of $70,507,075, on which it would have required a fraction over three per cent. taxes to pay the expenses of the State government, under the provisions of that constitution, to say nothing about county and Federal taxation. Prior to the war, the current rate of taxation was about one-half per cent. But when the whole complex element of change is fully understood and appreciated, as to the depreciation of real property in South Carolina since the war, and the constantly lessening resources of the people to meet this increasing annual drain upon them, the difference is still greater and more striking; as, for example, take an item of real estate worth before the war $20,000. The one-half per cent. of taxation before the war would be the sum of $100. Under the rate of taxation fixed by the constitution, it would require the sum of $600 to pay the taxes on the same property. The relative proportions for the two periods would stand as one to six. But even this statement does not cover all the contingencies of value and taxation. The property valued before the war at $20,-000 has now only a value of $6,000. Before the war a tax of one-half per cent. upon its latter valuation would produce the sum of only $30; but to realize the $600, would require a taxation at the rate of ten per cent., so that, taking into joint consideration the depreciation of the property, and the great increase in the rate of taxation, the proportion will, in fact, stand as one to twenty.

On this subject we have the following testimony of Judge Carpenter:

Question. State how the tax on the real estate of South Carolina is imposed; what it is now as compared with what it was four years ago. State your general knowledge in regard to taxation in the State.

Answer. The property is assessed by the auditor of each county, and a return of the assessment is made to the State Auditor. The board of equalization then examines the returns from each county, and adds to or detracts from the amount at which the property is assessed. This board, without seeing the property or knowing any thing about it, receives complaints from persons assessed; or, if they think the assessment too low in a county, they do as they did in Orangeburg; they quadrupled the amount of taxation in Orangeburg; they said it was not enough.

Question. Without seeing the property at all?

Answer. Yes, sir; without seeing it. It was done by the board of equalization at Columbia. They made it four times what it had been assessed at, and they doubled it in a great many counties. There were a very few counties where they did not add something, and if they diminished it in any county I do not know where. The property of South Carolina is assessed and taxed in round numbers at $180,000,000. I do not think it would sell in any market for $100,000,000, for South Carolina has vast tracts of poor land. I think property is assessed there at about twice its value.

Question. On an average ?

Answer. Yes, sir. I will instance one case in Clarendon, where a tract of land had been offered two years for $5,000, and they assessed it at $15,000, and the owner could not get the board of equalization to do any thing about it. Taxes seemed to be assessed with a view to the supposed necessities of the State for revenue, rather than to the value of property.

Question. A sweeping assessment made in particular localities, without any knowledge of the property at all ?

Answer. Yes, sir. The tax assessed upon South Carolina this year for State purposes is over $4,000,000.

Question. For State purposes alone ?

Answer. The State tax is over $4,000,000 this year.

Question. Up to 1866 and 1867, what was the general taxation in South Carolina for State purposes ?

Answer. I could not tell you any thing about 1866 and 1867, for we were then under a military government. Prior to the war, the taxable property of the State was about $480,000,000, against $180,000,000 now; and I think the taxes raised for State purposes averaged about $400,000.

Question. And the tax is now about ten times that much ?

Answer. Well, I must state, in justice to all parties, when I say that the tax is over $4,000,000 this year for State purposes, that they have crowded two years into one. Of course the tax for last year was due and collectable by law this year. The Legislature passed an act making this year's taxes due and collectable this year also. It was a different system from that we have had. When I say that over $4,000,000 is levied this year for State taxes, I mean to say that they are trying to collect two years' taxes in one.

Question. In the present condition of the State, what effect has that upon the property of the people?

Answer. It is very depressing.

By Mr. VAN TRUMP:

Question. How do you account for the state of facts which you say exists in relation to your taxes?

Answer. Some property is taxed about right, but others five times too much.

Question. Is that a matter of favoritism toward certain people, or how is it?

Answer. I will state the facts, and leave you to draw your own inference. There is a committee, or a board, appointed, tax commissioners I think they are called; a board of equalization; they receive the reports of the county assessors, and then they decide that such a man must pay so much on his land, and another man pay so much on his.

Question. Is this board of equalization frequently made up of negroes?

Answer. I believe most of them are negroes. They meet together, and, without seeing anybody at all, decide that such a man must pay so much and another man so much. The way it is so unequally distributed is this: Adjoining plantations are sometimes very different in value, as you all know. A man may own a plantation on a large creek or river, and it may be worth twenty dollars an acre; while his neighbor may own an adjoining plantation, but it may be of poor land not worth one dollar an acre.

But this board of equalization cannot tell those facts; they are there in their office, and merely make out their statements, and decide that the tax must be so much, and it has to be paid. And in that way a man who has a plantation worth $30,000 may not pay any more tax than the man whose plantation is only worth $5,000.

CHAPTER XXXII.

On the Character of the Low-Country Negro.

THE following testimony was elicited by the congressional committee in regard to the character and capacity of the low-country negro, from two gentlemen of standing and experience.

Judge Carpenter, of South Carolina, speaks as follows :

Question. Of course you have been quite familiar with the negro population of South Carolina. How do they compare in intelligence with the colored population of the border States, such as the colored population of Maryland and Kentucky? I know you are familiar with the colored population of Kentucky, as well as myself. How does the colored population of South Carolina compare in intelligence with the colored population in these States; and, if they are less intelligent, what, in your opinion, is the cause of it?

Answer. If you except a portion of the colored population of the city of Charleston—

Question. I mean outside of cities?

Answer. Except a portion of the old colored population there, that have been free for a long period of years, a great many of whom are people of intelligence, good character, reputation for probity and honesty, and even men of property—if you except them, the rest are very much less enlightened than the colored people of the border States. However, the farther you move north in the State, the nearer you approach the mountains, and, in the mountains themselves, they are more intelligent than on the sea-coast or on the rivers. The colored population upon the sea-coast and upon the rivers, in point of intelligence, is just as slightly removed from the animal creation as it is conceivable for a man to be. I venture to say that no gentleman here would be able to understand one of them upon the witness-stand, or would be able to know what he meant. I have had to exercise more patience and more ingenuity in that particular, to have more explanations and interpretations, to find out what a witness meant to say, who had witnessed a murder, for instance, than to understand any thing else in my life. They talk a very outlandish idiom, utterly unknown to me. They are very ignorant, and still have very strong passions, and these bad men lead them just as a man would drive or lead a flock of sheep.

Question. That brings me to the question which I desired to ask, whether or not that character of population, ignorant and degraded as you have described them, are not very easily controlled and led by persons who acquire their confidence?

Answer. Very easily. They believe any thing they are told, no matter how ridiculous. As an instance of that I will say, that two of the most serious charges made against me by the colored population when I was a candidate for Governor were, first, that if I was elected I would reduce them again to slavery; and, second, failing to do that, I would not allow their wives and daughters to wear hoop-skirts.

Question. How did they get the latter idea?

Answer. It does not matter how ridiculous a thing is; they believe any thing. They are a very credulous set. Those men have as absolute control over them as any slave-holder ever had over his slaves before slavery was abolished.

Question. In what way did they obtain and maintain that sort of control?

Answer. They obtained the control originally by the white people of South Carolina refusing to take any part in the elections in the organization of the State. These men then went to the colored people and said, "We are your friends; we are going into this thing, and have you educate your children, and make every thing better for you," and all that sort of thing. They got their confidence and control. The white people did not go among them. The colored people in that way were made inimical to the white people, and led to think that their interests were antagonistic to the interests of the white people. The white people held the property and what little money there was. The colored people were taught by these men to believe that the lands properly belonged to them, and not to their former masters; that the dwelling-houses, and gin-houses, and every thing else, belonged to them. I heard that repeatedly stated on the stump last summer, not only by colored men, but by white men. Senator Beverly Nash, a colored man, at Columbia, a very shrewd, sharp, keen man, in a public speech to six or eight thousand men, said to them: "The reformers complain of taxes being too high. I tell you that they are not high enough. I want them taxed until they put these lands back where they belong, into the hands of those who worked for them. You toiled for them, you labored for them, and were sold to pay for them, and you ought to have them." That was the key-note of the whole stumping, from the sea-coast to the mountains. Some of the people did not say any thing about it; but it was a fierce contest, from beginning to end, to array race against race. Our efforts were directed to harmonize the two races for political purposes and legal purposes.

General John B. Gordon, lately elected United States Senator from Georgia, said :

Those negroes upon the coast are very different from the negroes in Middle and Upper Georgia; they are almost an entirely different race of people. They are excessively ignorant. The intelligence of the negro in the middle and upper counties of Georgia is very much the same as the intelligence of the negro here or anywhere over the country. But in the southern portion of the State, where there is a large negro belt, as we call it, the negroes have absolutely a language of their own. If a negro from Washington were to talk with a negro from Atlanta, or the upper portion of Georgia, their language would be the same; they would use about the same words to express the same ideas. But it is not so on the coast. If a negro were transported from this city to the coast of Georgia, he would not understand at all a great deal that many of the negroes of that coast would say. Their old masters, who grew up with them, do understand their language; but it is a peculiar language. It is different from the language of the negroes in any other portion of our State, or any other portion of the South, except along the Atlantic belt.

Question. Is that class of negroes still there?

Answer. They are there now, and in very large numbers, upon the Sea Islands and upon the rice-plantations. They are very ignorant. They are entirely different from

12

the negroes from the middle section of the State upward.
The latter are much more intelligent than those along the
sea-coast.

Question. As to those negroes along the black belt, whom
you have described as having their own peculiar language
and religious superstitions, with what sort of intelligence
do they seem to exercise the right of suffrage? How are
they controlled and managed?

Answer. Well, sir, they had just begun voting when I
left there; they were at that time, and are still, so far as
my knowledge of the State extends—I know it is true of a
large portion of the State—controlled almost entirely by
the League organizations. The negroes were introduced
very early into what they called the Union Leagues; and
they were controlled by those Leagues. They seemed to be
under the impression that by voting they were to acquire
some sort of property, and were influenced mainly by ideas
of that sort, which had been instilled into them by these
people who had gone there among them. I, however,
know less about the particular influence brought to bear
now, in that part of the State, with regard to voting, than
in any other part, because I have been in that portion
of the State less since they have been voting. When I
left there they had just commenced voting.

We append to these views some hopeful observations made in the Tax-payers' Convention
in 1871, which reflect the sentiments of many
worthy people. Mr. Dudley said:

The day is fast approaching when the native Carolinian
and the colored man will be in perfect accord in all measures for their mutual protection, and the thirty thousand
votes which have spread such ruin over the State will turn
their batteries against those who have selfishly destroyed

the people to enrich themselves, and make the colored race poorer still, who were poor enough before. As a race, they are kind-hearted and affectionate, and desire to lean upon those with whom they played in their childhood.

With natures thus inclined, our task of perfect reconciliation is easy. Let us be not only just to them, but generous. The obligation is upon us. They gave us their work during the war, when an obvious self-interest might have stimulated their hostility. They protected our families by all the means in their power, when the white man was on the distant battle-field, and his home was without other protectors. Surely, if ever there was a debt, founded on the strongest moral obligation, it will be found in the humble claims which the colored man now makes upon his former owners, and this is, only that they may be protected in the rights which the results of the war have given them—rights, which they never demanded for themselves, but have only accepted at the hands of others.

Upon this easy condition, this thirty thousand majority, heretofore hostile, will melt away, as a huge glacier under the warming rays of the sun. It may not be the work of a moment, but the result is only a question of time. Already is it commenced, and the relations between the races are now far more cordial than they have ever been since the war. Now, let this convention, composed as it is of the heroes of many a battle-field, rise up to the moral heroism of proclaiming to the world their unalterable purpose to repay the kindness and fidelity of the colored man by an unreserved acknowledgment of his newly-acquired rights, and such a pledge, coming from the representative men of South Carolina, who have never yet learned to equivocate or evade, will be respected by all those who are capable of appreciating properly the obligations of personal honor.

CHAPTER XXXIII.

Southern Sentiment since the War.

It is an injurious and unfounded supposition, which is the cause of much prejudice at the North, that there is still a considerable body of people in the South who are passionately inimical to the Government, and who would, if they could, break up the existing state of things and restore slavery.

We have elsewhere stated our convictions that a large majority of the Southern people never wanted to break up the Union and never wanted war, and that this great body stands firm to-day for peace, union, and emancipation, reënforced by an immense proportion of that remainder who advocated secession. The traveler in the South will inquire long and often before he will find a man who will advocate the restoration of slavery. Such a one we have never found. The great body of public sentiment on this question is undoubtedly echoed in the views expressed in the Carolina Tax-payers' Convention on several occasions, from which there was never any dissent. They were briefly expressed by Mr. Trenholm in the following language :

The people of the South stood up manfully during the war, in the defence of their principles. They believed slavery to be an institution founded by the Author of all good, for wise and gracious purposes; the pious and good entertained that belief; and, feeling their high responsibility, struggled against the sentiment of the world. And, sir, when that same Providence in an unexpected hour, and in an unexpected manner, relieved us from this great charge, the people of this State acquiesced in its decree. No man believes that the restoration of slavery in this country is possible or desirable. If such a possibility did exist, and it were ever submitted to the vote of this convention, my conviction is that not a voice would be raised in its favor.

The testimony of General Grant, who went South after the war, has been too little heeded. In his report to President Johnson he said:

HEADQUARTERS ARMIES OF THE UNITED STATES.)
    WASHINGTON, D. C., *December* 18, 1865. (

To his Excellency ANDREW JOHNSON,
    President of the United States.

SIR: In reply to your note of the 16th inst., requesting a report from me, giving such information as I may be possessed of, coming within the scope of the inquiries made by the Senate of the United States in their resolution of the 12th inst., I have the honor to submit the following:

With your approval, and also that of the honorable Secretary of War, I left Washington City on the 27th of last month for the purpose of making a tour of inspection through some of the Southern States, or States lately in rebellion, and to see what changes were necessary to be made in the disposition of the military forces of the country; how these forces could be reduced and expenses cur-

tailed, etc., etc., and to learn, as far as possible, the feelings and intentions of the citizens of those States toward
the General Government.

·　　·　　·　　·　　·　　·　　·

Both in traveling and while stopping I saw much, and
conversed freely with the citizens of those States, as well
as with officers of the army who have been stationed
among them.

The following are the conclusions come to by me:

I am satisfied that the mass of the thinking men of
the South accept the present situation of affairs in good
faith. The questions which have heretofore divided the
sentiment of the people of the two sections—slavery and
State-rights, or the right of a State to secede from the
Union—they regard as having been settled forever by the
highest tribunal—arms—that man can resort to.

I was pleased to learn from the leading men whom I
met, that they not only accepted the decision arrived at as
final, but, now the smoke of battle has cleared away, and
time has been given for reflection, that this decision has
been a fortunate one for the whole country, they receiving
like benefits from it with those who opposed them in the
field and in council.

·　　·　　·　　·　　·　　·　　·

The presence of black troops, lately slaves, demoral-
izes labor, both by their advice and by furnishing in their
camps a resort for the freedmen for long distances around.
White troops generally excite no opposition, and therefore
a small number of them can maintain order in a given district. Colored troops must be kept in bodies sufficient to
defend themselves. It is not the thinking men who would
use violence toward any class of troops sent among them
by the General Government, but the ignorant in some places
might; and the late slave seems to be imbued with the idea

that the property of his late master should by right belong to him, or at least should have no protection from the colored soldier. There is danger of collisions being brought on by such causes.

My observations lead me to the conclusion that the citizens of the Southern States are anxious to return to self-government within the Union as soon as possible; that while reconstructing they want and require protection from the Government; that they are in earnest in wishing to do what they think is required by the Government, not humiliating to them as citizens; and that, if such a course were pointed out, they would pursue it in good faith. It is to be regretted that there cannot be a greater commingling at this time between the citizens of the two sections, and particularly of those intrusted with the law-making power.

.   .   .   .   .   .

U. S. GRANT,
Lieutenant-General.

There has never been any reason, since the writing of the foregoing letter, to show that any modification of its judgment is required to express the facts of the situation from that time to this. There certainly never was a civil war ended in which there were fewer after-claps than in ours.

We quote a single item of testimony from the congressional committee's report, that is valuable on the point of whether the Southern people wanted to go to war, which is elsewhere discussed. The committee say:

The leaders, having supreme power at home, could not

bear to lose control of the national Government. They
rebelled, and drew the masses with them.

The common people tell us they did not want to fight,
but were obliged to follow their leaders. The same ruling
classes in other States, having produced a similar condition
of society, though none so bad, were for secession; the
people held back until South Carolina precipitated war.
Then the leaders in other States urged the people not to
abandon a "sister State," and State after State was hurled
into the conflict, the people knowing not now. Plain men
all over the South tell us they did not desire disunion nor
war, but were compelled to follow their "great leaders,"
and go "with their States" and with "the South." It
was the system of government which prevailed in these
States, but most perfectly in South Carolina, based on
slavery, with authority in the hands of a few, which caused
the war, with all its losses of blood and treasure.

Is it not time to bring to an end the punishment of the innocent many for the crimes of the
guilty few?

CHAPTER XXXIV.

On the Labor Question.—Labor abundant and cheap.—Its Tendency to reorganize itself.—A Field for Philanthropic Exertion.

AGRICULTURAL labor is abundant in South Carolina, and can be had by anybody, who is willing to pay even less than a fair price for it. The general impression that the old slave was indolent, loitering, and lazy, is not well founded. No man can be a witness to his movements in the field without seeing that he is the best of workers. Men and women alike are vigorous, quick and athletic. The chief complaint of the freedman as a laborer is that he is inconstant. The testimony of the managers of the phosphate-works about Charleston, who employ many of them, is, that they average about four days' labor in the week. This is where they have the attractions of the town to distract them. In the country, where there are no shows and no whisky-shops, the temptations to vagrancy are less, and the laborers are more steady.

We have elsewhere shown how profitable

cotton-culture can be made in the vicinity of the
large towns.   It is the simple fact that good hus-
bandry will produce the results exhibited, that
demonstrates the profitableness of South Carolina
farming.   These results can be obtained anywhere, or a near approximation to them, wherever
there is good management.   The commercial fer-
tilizers in the market produce almost the same
result as the stable manures.   Guano, and the
phosphates now dug in such abundance from the
soil in the neighborhood of Charleston, answer
nearly every demand of high and productive cultivation.   At all events, they furnish an adequate
basis for them.   The question of successful and
profitable cotton-culture thus becomes mainly a
question of labor.

It is an important fact which must not be overlooked, that, in the South, as in the farming districts of Europe, a large proportion of the work
is done by females, whose labor in many cases is
as valuable as that of the men.   A woman will
hoe as much cotton, and pick as much, as a man.
And the same may be said of other field-work.
In a cotton-field to-day there were ten hands at
work; six were women and four were men.
They were ploughing, trenching, manuring, and
preparing for the seed.   The women carried the
raw stable-manure from the heaps in baskets on
their heads, and spread it in the drills.   It was

evident they were as efficient workers as the men, as active and as strong. The work was in this case being done by the day, and was rapidly and faithfully performed. Under the old slave-system, labor was so systematized as to secure the greatest amount of work, and leave the smallest margin for shirking. A dozen ploughs, for example, were set in motion in a field; the file leader being a first-rate hand, all were required to follow with equal celerity and thoroughness. It was the same in other branches of farm-work. In hoeing and picking a certain stint was often given, which afforded little time for idleness. The foreman to-day in the field volunteered the remark that the women can and do both hoe and pick more cotton than the men, and with less fatigue to themselves. He added, "I never saw the day when I could hoe as much cotton as my wife there." The common stint is to hoe an acre; now, anybody who goes over an acre of ground with a hoe in a day, we may be sure will have few idle moments. The negro, male and female, has been used to pushing work ahead under the eye of drivers and overseers, and the result is what we have depicted.

The Columbia cotton-raisers do not complain of their field-hands. They can and do obtain plenty of excellent laborers at low wages. They only have a way of saying that the blacks have to be looked after, as if any laborers did not. But they admit they prefer hiring their people by the day, instead of by piece or stint work. They can procure any number for occasional or steady labor for half a dollar a day here in Columbia, the laborers feeding themselves. The wages of the men hired by the year are one hundred dollars per annum, and "found" by the hirer. At these rates labor is abundant in Columbia, and they are the basis of prices in the rural districts.

But there is this complaint, that, while it is easy enough to obtain laborers in the towns, it is not so easy to do it in the country. This is probably true. It is true everywhere; but the fault is not with the workman any more than it is with the employer. The black man is expected to perform a large amount of toil for a small sum of money; to put up with the meanest habitations, and, where he is fed by his employer, with the most meagre fare. In a word, he is expected to be content to be housed as in the days of slavery, and to be restricted to the old plantation rations. There is no care or thought for the material comforts of the black man or woman. It is easy to see, from the artless conversation of the rural population, how little they get, and how little they expect. It is equally plain how inexacting and well disposed they are as a class, and how much they would appreciate fair treatment.

There seems to be no reason to doubt that an ample supply of faithful and steady laborers could be readily obtained by any man who would honestly undertake to farm in South Carolina, on righteous principles, giving the negro such food and such shelter as the dictates of an enlightened self - interest and a humane spirit would prompt, and that this supply could be obtained at the most reasonable rates.

The truth is, that the largest half of the population of South Carolina live to-day in huts and hovels, so poor that their total destruction, from one end of the State to the other, would not diminish the taxable values of the State one-tenth of one per cent. They are worth no more than so many dog-kennels or pigsties. Under any system which looks to putting the agricultural interests of the State on a permanent footing, here is one of the first things to be remedied, and the improvement would not involve any serious charge. Sawed lumber is worth less to-day in the interior of both the Carolinas than in the State of Maine, and colored mechanics abound.

We judge there is not a better opportunity in the world to organize agricultural labor on a paying basis to the employer, and a satisfactory one to the employed, than exists here to-day. To show how tractable is the material, and how encouraging the prospect, it is only necessary to point to the methods already existing on some of the old plantations. In some cases twenty or more families of the old slaves combine and agree to pay the owner so much money for the use of the land. They work harmoniously, and divide harmoniously at the end of the year. In one such instance the little colony had bought several hundred acres of plantation-land out of their surplus savings, and were beginning cultivation as proprietors. This embryonic community system has sprung naturally from the situation, and already unlocks several of its difficulties, and opens a cheerful prospect of still further ameliorations. Cotton-culture is such an easy means of bringing into service the entire agricultural population, including the women and children, that the reorganization of labor is not at all difficult. This fact, and the habits of field-work thus engendered, put the agriculture of this region on a totally different footing from that of the North, and assimilate it to that of the best-cultivated foreign countries, where it is made so productive and profitable.

Philanthropy could hardly find a more praiseworthy field for its exertions, or one more likely to repay them in material returns, than to establish a model plantation in South Carolina, and so demonstrate what can be done with this black free labor, on a system of paying good wages, and of supplying good food and comfortable shelter to the laborers. That the blacks would feel a lively appreciation of such an effort in their behalf, cannot admit of any doubt. The benefits of a successful example of this sort would be beyond computation. By first eliminating the best portions of the colored population and improving their physical condition, it would pave the way for their social and moral elevation; and thus perhaps might be laid the foundation of a revolution in the character of the race, that would lead to the most benignant results.

THE END.

Printed in the United States
143306LV00002BA/54/A

9 781933 706030